THE MURDER OF GEORGE MOSCONE

First edition. July 16, 2021.

Copyright © 2021 Ruth Kanton.

ISBN: 979-8215049013

Written by Ruth Kanton.

THE MURDER OF GEORGE MOSCONE

1

RUTH KANTON

The Milk-Moscone Assassinations
George Moscone

George Moscone was born on November 24, 1929, to George Joseph Moscone, a milk wagon driver, and Lena Moscone, a homemaker. Following his parents' separation, Moscone and his mother settled in Cow Hollow District, and she took up various jobs to support herself and her son. Moscone attended Catholic schools, St. Brigid's then St. Ignasius High School, where he excelled in the debate team and was an all-star basketball player. He graduated as a lawyer from University of California, Hastings School of the Law. In 1954, Moscone married Gina Bondanza, whom he had met while they were in grade school. After a brief stint in the United States Navy, he opened his own private practice in 1956.

Moscone was a close friend of John L. Burton, who he had met in 1947. John's older brother, Phillip Burton, was a member of the California State Assembly in 1960, when he recruited Moscone to run for an Assembly seat on the Democrat ticket. By this time, Moscone was known as a progressive, liberal Democrat, having worked in various political positions, including registering black voters in Mississippi. However, Moscone lost the Assembly seat. His political ambitions were sparked, and in 1963, he won a seat on the San Francisco Board of Supervisors. He was an outspoken supervisor, often championing for the needs of the poor people, racial minorities and small business owners. In 1966, Moscone set his sights on the California State Senate, and won a seat representing the 10th District in San Francisco County. In the California Democratic Party, Moscone rose through the ranks quickly, and was affiliated with the progressive San Francisco politicians. He was elected Majority Leader soon after his State Senate win.

In 1970, he was reelected to the State Senate representing the 10th District and in 1974 he was elected to the 6th District seat, which had been newly redistricted. Moscone had set his eye on the California Governor seat in 1974, but quickly dropped out when he realized that he had slim to none chances of defeating California Secretary of State Jerry Brown. Moscone announced that he would be running for the San Francisco Mayoral seat on December 19, 1974. In the November 1975 close race, Moscone emerged the winner, ahead of Conservative City Supervisor John Barbagelata, with Dianne Feinstein taking third place. In the runoff election held in December, Moscone won the seat, beating Barbagelata by less than 5,000 votes. He was 46 years old at the time, and a father of four children – Jennifer, Rebecca, Christopher, and Jonathan.

Harvey Milk

Harvey Milk was born on May 22, 1930, to William Milk and Minerva Karns in Woodmere, New York City. At Bay Shore High School, Milk was known as the class clown, often teased about his big nose, protruding ears and oversized feet. He played football, and was passionate about opera. Following his high school graduation on 1947, Milk joined New York State College for Teachers, now State University for New York, and majored in Mathematics. After his graduation in 1951, Milk joined the United States Navy during the Korean War, serving as a diving officer aboard USS *Kittiwake*, a submarine rescue ship. He was then transferred to San Diego's Naval Station to serve as a diving instructor. Milk was discharged from the Navy in 1955 as a lieutenant, junior grade.

Milk knew he was gay from an early age, but kept his sexual orientation a secret from friends and family. Following his discharge from the Navy, he found a job as a high school teacher in George W. Hewlett High School in Long Island. In 1956, Milk pursued Joe Campbell, a man six years younger than him, relentlessly. They had met at Jacob Riis Park beach in Queens, a popular hangout spot for gay men at the time. Milk and Campbell moved in together, and after a while, got bored with New York. They moved to Dallas, Texas, but only lived in the state for a short while. Bored and unhappy, they moved back to New York. Back in New York, Milk began working at an insurance company as an actuarial statistician. After six years, Milk and Campbell broke up. This was Milk's longest relationship.

After abruptly quitting his job at the insurance firm, Milk joined Bache & Company, a Wall Street firm, as a researcher. He was outspoken and eclectic, and tended to offend the older members of the firm by flaunting his success and ignoring their advice. Despite his problems with colleagues, he was often promoted. In 1962, he began dating Craig Rodwell, who was 10 years younger. However, Rodwell was a member of the gay-rights organization Mattachine Society, and his affinity for antagonizing police was something Milk couldn't handle. They broke up soon after.

Move to San Francisco

In 1964, Milk began a relationship with Jack Galen McKinley, who was 16 years old at the time. Milk was a Goldwater Republican at the time, and recruited McKinley to work on Barry Goldwater's 1964 presidential campaign. By 1969, McKinley had begun working as a stage manager for Broadway director Tom O'Horgan. When the Broadway touring company of *Hair* moved to San Francisco, Milk and McKinley also packed up and relocated to San Francisco. By this time, Milk was disillusioned by his job, with his colleagues noticing that his heart was not in the job despite the fact that he was really good at it. Once they made their move to San Francisco, Milk fell in love with the city. His relationship with McKinley, however, was getting worse. They finally broke up when McKinley was offered a job in New York for the production of *Jesus Christ Superstar*. In San Francisco, Milk got a job in an investment firm. However, following the United States invasion of Cambodia, he grew even more disillusioned with the political climate. He began growing his hair out, and when he was asked to cut it, he refused. This got him fired from his job. Milk drifted aimlessly for a while, moving from California to Texas to New York without any plans or a steady job. He finally joined O'Horgan's theater company as a "general aide."

Milk met Scott Smith, a man 18 years younger, and the two began a relationship. They decided to move to San Francisco, and settled in Castro Street, a neighborhood that was popular with the gay community. They lived off their savings, and using their last $1,000, opened a camera store on Castro Street in March 1973. His interest in politics peaked after his experience with various policies and civic problems. He ran for city supervisor in 1973, but lost. However, his flamboyant speeches and media skills garnered him extensive attention. He was deeply involved in the issues of Castro Street, often helping out small businesses and forming coalitions to solve various problems. Castro Camera became the center of various neighborhood activities, and Milk was dubbed the "Mayor of Castro Street."

City Supervisor Win

Milk ran for the city supervisor spot in 1975 again, and came in seventh, one spot away from a win. During the second election run, Milk decided to quit smoking marijuana, cut off his hair, and vowed to never visit gay bathhouses again. His changes were aimed at getting him taken seriously as a candidate, and it seemed to have the desired effect. He championed for the causes of small business owners on Castro Street, which spiked his popularity in the area. Following his Mayoral win in 1975, George Moscone met with Milk at Castro Camera, and promised Milk an appointment as city commissioner. True to his word, Moscone appointed Milk to be Board of Permit Appeals in 1976. However, Milk only served five weeks on the board. He was fired after announcing his plans to run for the California State Assembly. In the Assembly elections, Milk lost to Art Agnos by less than 4,000 votes.

Following his loss, Milk set his sights back on the city supervisor seat. In November 1976, voters in San Francisco decided to stop using the citywide ballot for supervisor elections, instead opting for district ballot. With this policy change, seventeen candidates emerged for District 5, encompassing Castro Street and its environs. Milk quickly became the leading candidate in the district. Following the November 8, 1977, elections, Milk emerged victorious, securing a 30% lead against the other sixteen candidates.

Dan White

Daniel James White was born on September 2, 1946, in Long Beach, California. He was the second child of nine, and was raised in San Francisco's Visitacion Valley neighborhood. He came from an Irish-Catholic working family. He was an all-city football player in Riordan High School, but was expelled from the school for fighting in his junior year. He enrolled in Woodrow Wilson High School, and his performance at the school was exemplary, and he graduated as valedictorian of his class.

Following his graduation, White decided to enlist in the United States Army in June 1965. From 1969 to 1970, he served in the Vietnam War as a sergeant in the 101st Airborne Division. In 1971, he was honorably discharged from the Army. White then relocated to Anchorage, Alaska, where he found a job as a security guard at A. J. Dimond High School in 1972. White moved back to San Francisco and became a police officer. However, he ended up quitting the force after he refused to adhere to the police code of "solidarity." According to an account by the *SFWeekly*, White had stopped a fellow officer from beating up a black prisoner who had been handcuffed at the time. A straight-arrow, White went on to file a report naming the officer involved, something that was not done by officers at the time. Ray Sloan, a political consultant, stated: "His commanding officer begged him not to file the report, but he did it anyway. Dan had a very strong sense of fairness."

After exiting the police force, White joined the fire academy in 1974. At the time, under a federal consent decree, the San Francisco Fire Department was required to hire more minorities. However, in a bid to circumvent the requirement, the department would actually allow African Americans into the academy but then come up with ways to flunk them, usually through the written examinations. When three black students at the academy were about to be flunked out, White stood up for them, and began circulating a petition to let them remain in the academy. He personally worked to help them pass the exams, tutoring them after classes. A stellar student, White graduated valedictorian from the academy. As a firefighter, White was featured in the *San Francisco Chronicle* after he saved a woman and her child from a seventh floor apartment in the Geneva Towers in Visitacion Valley.

Run for Supervisor Seat

In the summer of 1977, White launched a campaign for District 8's supervisor seat. He was one of 13 candidates, and like many of the others, he was a novice in the political scene. However, he had various advantages over the other candidates. First, he was a former police officer, and this set him apart because of the high crime rate in the district. Additionally, of all the candidates, White was the only one who campaigned in the Sunnyvale projects. He would make his way down to the projects during the weekends and play tackle football with members of the Sons of Sunnyvale, a street gang. The Sons later began campaigning for White, distributing his campaign materials and attending his functions. When other candidates complained about the boisterous members of the Sons at events, White refused to ask them not to attend the functions. "These guys were part of his district and they had every right to participate, and they were dedicated to Dan," Sloan later told *SFWeekly*. The Moscow fire station also gave White an advantage over the other candidates. The firefighters would always cover White's shifts so that he could campaign in the precincts, and also stuffed mailboxes and handed out brochures. With the combined efforts of the fire station and the Sons of Sunnyvale, White was able to disseminate information faster than the other candidates. "We could write, print, and deliver within 24 hours. It's a huge advantage when you can do that and nobody else could," Sloan, who worked on White's campaign, recalled.

Following the November 8, 1977, elections, White emerged victorious. He joined an unprecedented diverse Board of Supervisors. In addition to Harvey Milk, the first openly gay man on the board, the board included Ella Hill Hutch, the first African American on the board, Carol Ruth Silver, the first single mother and feminist on the board, and Gordon Lau, the first Chinese American on the board.

With the city charter's prohibition that no one could hold two city jobs simultaneously, White left his position as a firefighter for the $9,600 a year city supervisor role.

Moscone: Mayor of San Francisco

Once he became mayor of San Francisco, George Moscone hit the ground running. The San Francisco Giants had been posting the lowest baseball attendance numbers for three consecutive seasons, from 1974 to 1976. Meanwhile, in Toronto, Paul Godfrey – who had become the chairman of Metro Toronto in 1973 – and Doug McDougall – the president of Labatt Brewing Company – had been looking to relocate a baseball team to Toronto for years. After deals with teams like the Cleveland Indians had fallen through, they became serious about their deal with the Giants. According to McDougall, "We got into negotiations with moving the San Francisco Giants, and we went ahead with full negotiations in the fall of '74. We didn't have our partnership until the summer of '75. In the fall of '75, we got serious about San Francisco. We were at the stage of having to write checks around the end of December of '75."

For Godfrey, his aim was to just have a professional baseball team in the city. However, McDougall and Labatt Brewing Company had other goals. "At the time, our competitors were big breweries. We were number three in the pecking order. We were losing market share nationally. We were losing in Ontario and further into it, we were losing in Ontario because we were losing in metro Toronto. We had a clear picture of what our problem was. It was to figure out how to turn the ship around in Ontario. It morphed into using sports as a vehicle to getting our name out there. We had done that very well in Manitoba with Labatt Pilsner and became associated with the Winnipeg Blue Bombers. The nickname became so popular that we changed the name of the brand to 'Blue.' We were looking for a vehicle in Toronto to do for us what the Blue Bombers did for us in Winnipeg," McDougall explained.

On January 9, 1976, the behind-the-scenes deal for the Toronto Giants was finally unveiled to the public. "We all gathered in Paul Godfrey's office. We all told the press and then the board approved the sale of the team to Labatt's, subject to approval of the team by the Major League owners. So, we made the announcement, January 9th on TV, we had the logos and everything with the 'Toronto Giants,'" McDougall stated. However, the move never materialized. Newly-elected mayor of San Francisco, George Moscone, was determined to stop the team from moving to Toronto. Moscone filed an injunction with the court to halt the sale of the San Francisco Giants, and he was granted a temporary injunction. With the sale halted, San Francisco businessman Bob Lurie got the opportunity to buy the team. In February 1976, he announced that he was placing an $8 million bid for the team, despite Labatt's $13.5 million bid. On March 2, 1976, Lurie's bid was unanimously accepted by the other National League club owners. Moscone had gotten his wish – The San Francisco Giants would remain in the Bay Area.

Moscone became the first mayor to create a greatly diverse city hall, appointing a large number of racial minorities, women, gays and lesbians to advisory boards and city commissions. He also appointed Charles Gain as the police chief, a move that sparked resentment from officers in the San Francisco Police Department. Gain had moved from the Oakland Police Department as its police chief, and was considered an outsider. Gain and Moscone became even unpopular among the police ranks after Gain proposed that the department settle a lawsuit filed by minorities which claimed discriminatory hiring practices by the department.

Moscone was also partly responsible for the passing of the Americans with Disabilities Act in 1990. When the group of over 100 Americans with disabilities occupied the San Francisco Federal Building in April 1977, Moscone decided to stand up against Washington. Instead of complying with the federal government's plan to starve out the occupants, Moscone arranged for portable showers and towels to be brought into the building, helping make the 25-day sit-in successful.

The Visitacion Valley Youth Center

While it seemed like Harvey Milk and Dan White would be at odds in the Board of Supervisors, the opposite was actually true. White was a Democrat, but his leaning was majorly conservative. Despite this, he was an unlikely supporter of Milk, even going as far as asking Dianne Feinstein, the board chairman, to appoint Milk as the chairman of the Streets and Transportation Committee. The two men would often vote in favor of each other's proposals, and their friendship developed outside the city hall. They would meet for coffee once a week just to talk, and Milk was one of only three board members invited to the christening of White's first baby. White would be criticized by his fellow conservative board members for voting in favor of gay rights, but he never backed down. He voted to save Pride Center, an establishment that served as a meeting location for gay seniors and veterans. Unfortunately, Milk and White's friendship came to an unfortunate end.

The Catholic Church put in a proposal with the board – they planned to build a Youth Center for juvenile offenders who had committed serious crimes, including rape, arson, and murder. The center was to be in the Portola neighborhood of District 8, White's jurisdiction, on a convent property. Even though he was Irish-Catholic,

White opposed the idea from the beginning. According to Ray Sloan, part of White's opposition stemmed from the fact that the church had bullied some of its parishioners in Portola, telling them that they would end up in hell if they did not support the creation of the facility. White kept working for the board's votes, highlighting the possibility that his already high-crime district would see a surge in serious crime with the new facility, putting the citizens at higher risk. On the Friday before church was to make its case before the board, White asked Sloan to take a head count of the likely votes. Sloan recalls Milk telling White, "Dan, you've really earned your $9,600 on this one."

Hearing this, White spent his weekend sure of his win against the Youth Center. However, when the board voted on the matter, Milk voted in favor of the facility, ensuring White's loss. White was left reeling from the loss, feeling humiliated and enraged. He blamed Milk for the loss and embarked on his retaliation.

Milk's Civil Rights Bill

Once he won his district's vote, Harvey Milk began his tenure by rallying support for the Civil Rights Bill that sought to ban discrimination in housing, employment, and public accommodations based on sexual preference. Talking about the bill, Milk stated: "This will be the most stringent gay rights law in the country. This one has teeth; a person can go to court if his rights are violated once this is passed." The gay community was thrilled by the bill, voicing their support. The bill received overwhelming support from the Board of Supervisors, with 10 of the 11 members voting in support of the bill. The only person who voted against the bill was Dan White. It seemed like he had finally enacted his retaliation, although it failed to work.

When asked about why he declined to support the bill, White stated that it was an "intrusion" into the city's private sector. "According to the city attorney's office, if a transvestite shows up at a private school with all the qualifications for teaching, they cannot refuse to hire him for an opening even if they object to having a man dressed as a woman in their school," he said, "respect the private rights of all people, including gays." He added that he feared that the residents who were upset by the "demands" of the "large minorities" like the city's homosexual community would leave or react punitively if the bill passed. While other supervisors did share the same concern, the campaigns lodged by the homosexual community helped the hesitant supervisors consider the bill as a civil rights issue and not merely as an endorsement of personal sexual preferences.

Following Milk's win with the ordinance, he went up against Proposal 6, also known as The Briggs Initiative. The ballot initiative sought to ban gays and lesbians from working in California's public schools. Sponsored by John Briggs, an Orange County state legislator, the bill received overwhelming opposition, with politicians like Milk, Governor Ronald Reagan, and President Jimmy Carter launching campaigns against it. Milk, particularly, was vocal about the bill, often making jokes to counter Briggs' argument. When Briggs would claim that the homosexual teachers only wanted to abuse their children, Milk countered by providing statistics that showed that pedophiles primarily identified as heterosexuals. When Briggs claimed that the children would want to mimic their teachers, Milk joked: "If it were true that children mimicked their teachers, you'd sure have a helluva lot more nuns running around." Unrelenting, Milk attended every single one of Briggs' events, and countered his arguments when he went throughout the state to speak against it. In the end, The Briggs Initiative lost by over one million votes. This was the apex of Milk's career.

White's Resignation

While Milk was thriving in his political career, White was floundering. He was faced with mounting financial problems, his $9,600 a year salary unable to support his young family. To try and make ends meet, he borrowed money and opened a fried potato stand at Pier 39. His wife Maryanne had quit her job as a teacher to take care of their child, and then had to work at the stand. The long hours and meager earnings took their toll on the family, and White began sinking into depression. He was disillusioned by how his work at city hall was going as he was unable to play the politics game well. Unable to cope, he handed in his resignation on November 10, 1978. On Monday, November 13, 1978, the Board of Supervisors officially accepted his resignation, and his nameplate was removed from the door to his former office.

However, losing White was not acceptable to the conservative special interest groups, the Chamber of Commerce, the police, and the firefighters. On November 14, 1978, White held continuous meetings with his aides and representatives from the other groups. He emerged from the meeting having changed his mind about the resignation. He asked Moscone for his job back, and Moscone agreed to rescind his letter of resignation and reappoint him. Harvey Milk, shocked by Moscone's decision, met with the mayor and asked him to think about the decision. This was their chance to get someone liberal on the board who would be on their side. During one of these conversations, White overheard Milk telling Moscone not to reinstate him.

On the night of Sunday, November 26, 1978, White received a call at his home. The caller, a reporter, wanted White's reaction to the news that he was not going to be reinstated. "No comment," White replied. Following his "resignation," White had started showing signs of severe depression. He felt sorry for himself, and would refuse to leave the house.

The Assassinations of George Moscone and Harvey Milk

George Moscone was set to announce White's replacement to the Board of Supervisors on Monday, November 27, 1978. He had ultimately decided to choose a more liberal candidate, federal housing official Don Horanzy.

In his home, Dan White showered, shaved and put on his best suit. He also picked up his .38 caliber Smith & Wesson Model 36 Chief's Special revolver, loaded with hollow-point bullets. He put 10 extra hollow-point shells in his pocket and asked a friend to drive him to city hall. At 10:14 a.m., about half an hour before Moscone's press announcement, White arrived at the Polk Street side of city hall. He walked into the front entrance, and that was when he saw the metal detectors. To circumvent them, he snuck into the building through a first floor window and made his way to Moscone's office. Moscone was in the inner office with Willie Brown, and White waited for Moscone's meeting to end. At 10:40 a.m., he walked into Moscone's office just as Brown left. The two talked for a while, with White inquiring whether he would be reinstated on the board. Moscone maintained that he would not, and White became agitated. When Moscone lit up a cigarette and offered White a drink as he tried to reason with him, White pulled out his gun and shot Moscone twice, hitting him in the shoulder and chest. After Moscone had dropped to the ground, White approached and holding the gun six inches from Moscone's head, fired two shots into his ear lobes, killing him instantly. White reloaded his weapon and walked out of Moscone's office.

As he walked down the hall looking for Milk, Dianne Feinstein called out to him, but he replied, "I have something to do first." He intercepted Harvey Milk, and asked for a moment of his time. They entered White's former office, and White immediately positioned himself in front of the door to block Milk's exit. He pulled out the revolver, and Milk immediately raised his hand to defend himself. The first bullet went through his wrist. White fired rapidly, hitting Milk twice in the chest and the fourth bullet hitting Milk's head. Once Milk was down, White stepped closer and shot him in the head again at close range. White then fled the scene.

Dianne Feinstein discovered Milk's body and called for help. She was then required to identify Mayor Moscone's body. In a press conference, Feinstein announced the shocking murders to the public: "As President of the Board of Supervisors, it's my duty to make this announcement. Both Mayor Moscone and Supervisor Harvey Milk have been shot and killed. The suspect is Supervisor Dan White."

Trial and Sentencing

Dan White turned himself in, walking into the northeast precinct he used to work it a few years earlier. He was transported to the homicide division in the hall of justice, and put into an interview room. Two inspectors were tasked with interviewing him, one being his good friend Frank Falzon. After 25 minutes of questions, White confessed to the murders. He cried during the confession and claimed that he had only gone to city hall to talk to Moscone.

Days following the confession, mourners attended Moscone's funeral service at St. Mary's Cathedral. He was buried at Holy Cross Cemetery in Colma, San Francisco. Harvey Milk was cremated, and his friends scattered his ashes in the waters beyond the Golden Gate Bridge.

On May 1, 1979, White's trial began. He had been charged with two counts of first-degree murder, and was facing the death penalty. His lawyer, Doug Schmidt, launched a diminished capacity defense. He hired four psychiatrists, including Dr. Martin Binder, to examine White. In his testimony in court, Dr. Binder discussed White's depression, and went on to talk about White's diet of junk food, Twinkies and Coca-Cola. Even though he spent little time discussing White's diet and its correlation to his depression, the media dubbed his testimony the "Twinkie Defense."

The prosecutors were convinced that they had a solid case, and proceeded to play White's confession tape in the courtroom. It did not take Frank Falzon long to realize that it had been a mistake. The jury, made up five men and seven women (five of the women were of the same age as White's mother, and were all Irish-Catholic), listened as White sobbed in the tape as he confessed. No less than four jurors began crying as they listened to the confession. The tape was an unforeseen disaster for the prosecution. Three weeks after the trial began, on May 21, 1979, after six days of deliberation, the jury returned a verdict – Dan White was guilty of voluntary manslaughter. He got a seven year and eight month sentence, sparking outrage in the city. The public, particularly the gay community, maintained that White had gotten away with murder, and this sparked the "White Night Riots."

Release and Suicide

After serving less than five years at Soledad Prison, White was released in January 1984. With the citizens of San Francisco still reeling and angry, Dianne Feinstein asked Police Chief Gain to visit White and discourage him from moving back to San Francisco. He agreed, and moved to Los Angeles.

However, he moved back to Visitacion Valley in 1985, and lived in his old home. On October 21, 1985, Frank Falzon responded to a crime scene in Visitacion Valley. He immediately recognized the address. When he arrived, he found a priest giving White the last rite, with two nuns praying as they knelt over his body. White had committed suicide in his garage by hooking up a hose from his exhaust pipe and into the car. He died of carbon monoxide poisoning.

Dan White was buried at Golden Gate National Cemetery in San Bruno, leaving behind his wife Maryann and their three children.

MURDER AND MARGARITAS THE TRUE STORY OF CYNTHIA GALENS

REBECCA BUTTONS

There are several major differences between female and male killers. For instance, women usually commit premeditated murders, planning each and every step prior to actually harming their victim. Women are also prone to poisoning their targets and doing it discreetly which could help them avoid punishment or discovery. They also rarely kill in a spur of the moment or because they enjoy it. Instead, there are at least several underlying reasons why women turn into murderers. One of them is self-preservation which could be true in the case of Cynthia Galens. She is a quiet woman who spent the majority of her life in a small community called Farmington in New York, doing her best to take care of her family.

She had two failed marriages when she met a veteran named Thomas Stack. Cynthia lost her job because of him but the connection was very strong, and the two moved in together instantly. Unfortunately, Thomas Stack battled addition and had some psychological problems which led him to be violent from time to time. Cynthia should have known about these since the couple did meet in a hospital but it seemed like she wasn't prepared well. Thomas Stack threatened Cynthia's daughter Emily which was something she couldn't stand. He was also violent towards her on some occasions.

Thomas Stack's death didn't surprise a lot of people when it happened. He was an alcoholic, and everyone suspected that he accidentally poisoned himself. But once the small town of Farmington heard that Cynthia was actually behind the murder and that she used a large amount of antifreeze to get rid of her husband, everyone was in pure shock. Cynthia was a lovely lady without prior charges, but she did complain a couple of times that Thomas Stack was hurting her in the privacy of her own home. Unable to cope with his mood swings, Cynthia claimed she wanted to make him ill so she could run away from the man himself. But the levels of antifreeze in his system told a different story – that the murder was premeditated and Cynthia could have saved the man's life if she told the truth in the hospital.

Early life

Cynthia Galens was born on February 7th, 1958 as Cynthia Stanton. She grew up in an all-American family, and like many girls from her generation, Cynthia met her first husband David Barber when she was in her twenties. The couple looked forward to their life together and wanted to start a family as soon as possible. They moved to Farmington, New York hoping to live there happily ever after. It was a small town, perfect for peaceful family life. Their son was born in 1986, and they named him Matthew. Unfortunately, Cynthia's happiness didn't last long, and David filed for a divorce soon after. David did not disappear from Matthew's life, and he took care of the boy as much as he could.

Cynthia moved on and fell in love with David Galens. She got married once again at the beginning of the 1990s, and the couple soon had a baby girl named Emily in 1992. But the second marriage didn't last long either. She separated from David but kept his last name. Repeating the same pattern, Cynthia maintained a friendly relationship with her second husband due to the fact that they had a daughter together and would speak to each other often. Emily lived with her mother while Matthew decided to spend the majority of his time with his father David Barber.

As a single mother Cynthia worked in many positions during the years she spent living in Farmington. The town is located near Rochester which opened up many possibilities for employment. She was an excellent housekeeper and liked that job very much. But when she heard about a position of clerical assistant at the Veterans Affairs hospital in Canandaigua, she signed up immediately. It was a step in the right direction for her. Unfortunately, she would face a huge tragedy in her life very soon. Her beloved son Matthew was only nineteen in October 2005 when he overdosed and died.

Matthew worked as a cook and was very excited to enroll in college next year. He was optimistic about his future but also had a dark side that included occasional usage of drugs. Matthew was at his father's house on the night he died, having fun with his friends all over town. It was later determined that he took a lethal combination of marihuana, cocaine, and prescription pills which stopped his heart. His father discovered Matthew's lifeless body in the morning, and there was nothing he could do to save him. After hearing about her son's death, Cynthia was devastated. She buried herself in work hoping to find some distraction from grieving. However, Cynthia was visibly depressed, and everyone could see that she was suffering greatly.

Hoping to find some emotional support, Cynthia started talking with one of the patients at the Veterans Affairs hospital she worked in. His name was Thomas Stack, and he was seeking treatment for his bipolar disorder, as well as alcoholism. He was born in Syracuse and served in the Marine Corps during the 1970s and 1980s. Thomas was then stationed in Travis Air Force Base in California where he was given a title of a senior airman. His troubles with alcohol started while he was in the army and continued throughout his entire life. It seemed that he knew exactly what Cynthia was going through and he was there for her. The two of them bonded quickly and started dating in secret. It was forbidden for the hospital staff to have a romantic relationship with one of the patients. Aware of the consequences, Cynthia and Thomas became an item. It took the hospital officials only a couple of months to find out about the affair and Cynthia was fired from her position. Thomas asked to be released from the hospital and he was invited to live with Cynthia and her teenage daughter Emily at their house in Farmington. Cynthia was aware of Thomas' alcoholism but she firmly believed that he got better. It didn't take Thomas too long to return to the bottle. He was admitted to hospitals several times during 2007 for alcohol abuse. Cynthia would take him back whenever he knocked on her door because Thomas simply didn't have anywhere to go. They would continue dating just like nothing happened.

Thomas Stack did have a dark side when he was drunk and Cynthia got to see it at least several times. The first major incident happened in January of 2008 when Thomas threatened to murder Cynthia's second husband as well as her daughter. He was very jealous of him and couldn't accept the fact that Cynthia still spoke to her former husband. On top of that, Emily was living with them in the same house, and Thomas couldn't stand it. Cynthia got worried because Thomas' threats started sounding serious. She reached for the phone to call the police. Concerned about her safety, Cynthia was granted a restraining order from a judge. But Thomas couldn't leave her alone, and he harassed her via phone all the time. He was them put in jail and was released three months after. Cynthia once again took him back, and they rekindled their relationship.

The abuse clearly continued afterward, and it was probably due to Thomas' alcoholism. It is unclear how many instances went unreported, but Cynthia did contact authorities once again in 2009. She claimed that Thomas physically attacked her by shoving her against a microwave in the kitchen, leaving her back bruised. The patrol car removed him from Cynthia's home and put him in the jail. Cynthia showed up at the station only a couple of days after the incident, offering money to bail Thomas out. Their relationship was obviously very toxic, but it seemed like they couldn't stay away from each other.

It is still unclear what made Cynthia go over the edge. While there was certainly a degree of abuse within her household, Thomas was her boyfriend and he was living in her house. She had a chance to walk away from him, but it seemed like she didn't want to. Things were about to escalate, and no one could have predicted the outcome.

The day of the poisoning

It was October 2nd, 2009 when Thomas bought himself a contained of pre-made margarita cocktail in a local store. Cynthia noticed what he brought in with the groceries and placed the beverage in a refrigerator. Knowing that he would go through the cocktail in a single night, she took antifreeze which is a toxic and dangerous chemical used for cars and poured it into a container. Antifreeze is poisonous to both humans and animals. It has a very sweet taste that can be difficult to notice, especially when combined with another drink. It has been used as a murder weapon in several cases. The process of dying from antifreeze ingestion is very painful because the poison works its way through the organism, affecting the organs one by one. Cynthia left the modified cocktail in the fridge and went to bed. When she woke up, Thomas was complaining that he was feeling ill. She brushed him off, continuing with her day. She had to visit her late son's grave, so Cynthia exited the house as soon as she got ready which was around noon.

Cynthia was back home at 04:00 PM and she found Thomas sitting in his armchair. At a first glance she thought he was sleeping because he was breathing heavily but once she got closer to him, Cynthia noticed foam all around his mouth. He couldn't wake up no matter how much she tried. Cynthia went to the refrigerator and saw that Thomas drank the entire gallon of a deadly margarita mix. It seemed like she didn't expect him to finish the container because Cynthia apparently got scared. Not knowing who to call, she phoned her ex-husband David Galens who was at her house in twenty minutes. The two of them tried to help Thomas on their own, but they were unsuccessful. David attempted CPR, but nothing could wake Thomas up. Realizing that something serious is at hand, David suggested they contact the paramedics. Once the ambulance arrived, they picked up Thomas and took him to the hospital. It was obvious that they had a serious situation in front of them. Cynthia didn't mention that she poured antifreeze into the man's drink. If she did, the doctors might have been able to save his life. Instead, they had no idea what was happening to the man.

Thomas was in excruciating pain for the next thirty hours. Doctors tried to help him, but they were in the dark about what was going on with their patient. Cynthia kept her mouth shut during this time, claiming that she was as oblivious as they were. Thomas Stack died in the hospital, and Cynthia still said nothing. The authorities didn't suspect any foul play having in mind that Thomas was a known alcoholic who suffered from bipolar disorder for decades. They thought he grew tired of his changing mood and finally decided to take his own life. Or perhaps it was an accident that led to the most tragic outcome. After all, alcoholics are known for drinking anything that has at least a little bit of alcohol in it when they are out of the real thing. It wouldn't be the first time the paramedics brought someone to the hospital who made a similar mistake. The doctors did the toxicology examination and they discovered he had traces of antifreeze in his system, but they suspected he drank it voluntarily. Cynthia was not accused of anything at that time, and she continued to live her life normally.

The discovery of the murder and the arrest

Cynthia was in the clear, and she acted like nothing major had happened in her life. Wanting a change of scenery, she decided to visit an old friend from her high-school days called Nancy Cothern who lived in Clearwater, Florida in January 2010 which was only a couple of months after Thomas' death. While she was down there, Cynthia opened up to her friend Nancy saying that she did poison her boyfriend with antifreeze and that his death wasn't an accident. Cynthia told the friend that she suffered greatly while they were together and that Thomas had abused her often. Cynthia's friend thought about her confession for a couple of days, thinking if the murder was justified or not. But she decided to contact the authorities, namely officer Darcy Hunt who was her acquaintance.

Darcy Hunt handled the situation professionally, talking to Cynthia first before taking any action. She did notice that the woman showed no remorse for what she had done to her boyfriend. Officer Hunt then told her superiors about Cynthia's confession, and they decided to contact New York Police with the information they had.

Cynthia was taken into custody by Clearwater Police Department and was sent to New York for further questioning. She repeated the story she told to officer Hunt without trying to change a single detail. But she did emphasize the fact that Thomas had physically abused her while he was drunk and that she simply couldn't take it any longer.

However, Cynthia claimed that she didn't mean to kill her boyfriend. Instead, she wanted to make him sick and unable to hit her. She knew that he would drink any alcoholic drink in the house, but he would definitely go for the margarita container first. While she didn't measure the exact amount of antifreeze she put into the cocktail, Cynthia was certain that the dose would not be lethal and that Thomas would feel slightly nauseated in the morning. Her exact words were: *"If I didn't want him around, I would've put a lot more in. I just wanted to get him sick."* Cynthia even admitted that she asked her daughter Emily to help her dispose of the body before calling her ex-husband. The teenager refused and was in shock to find out her mother actually attempted to kill Thomas. But no matter what she said in her interview, Cynthia Galens was facing a murder charge because she did take a man's life, by accident or not.

The trial

The trial was set to begin in autumn of 2010. Cynthia Galens pleaded not guilty in front of a judge during the preliminary hearing. She claimed that the whole thing was an accident and that she didn't want to hurt Thomas Stack. She told the judge the following: *"It's a horrible thing I did. I miss him so much I can't stand it. I'm the reason he's not here. He's not a good person sometimes, but nobody deserves that."* She was assigned to a defense lawyer named Matthew Mix who firmly believed that he could clear Cynthia of all charges. R. Michael Tantillo was at the head of the prosecution, and his team prepared a foolproof case with enough witnesses to lock Cynthia up for years.

Before the trial actually started in September 2010, Judge Kocher called Cynthia Galens and her attorney to offer her a plea deal. If she admitted that she was guilty of a second-degree murder, Cynthia would spend only eighteen years in prison. Cynthia and her lawyer didn't dwell on the offer too long. They immediately refused, saying that they want to take their chances and present Cynthia's case in front of a jury. Cynthia was certain that she had enough proof to convince everyone in the courtroom that she was actually Thomas' victim and that she didn't mean to murder him. Instead, she simply wanted to make him ill for a short amount of time.

On September 21st, 2010 Cynthia entered the courtroom followed by her attorney. The prosecution called their first witness - Nancy Cothern, Cynthia's high-school friend. After all, she was the one who alerted the authorities that the crime was committed and that Thomas Stack's death wasn't a suicide or an accident as it was assumed. Cothern recalled Cynthia's story adding that the woman was genuinely concerned about her and her daughter's safety while Thomas was in the house. She didn't forget the threats Thomas made a couple of years prior to the murder. However, Cothern did observe that Cynthia Galens didn't seem sorry for what she did while retelling the story. Cothern later told the reporters the following: *"The next day there was not any remorse what so ever, I think there was anger. I think she was angry at me, I think she was angry that now she knew that I was repeating it and that she wanted to leave with her daughter."* Nancy Cothern eventually broke the case by contacting Officer Darcy Hunt who was interested right away.

Officer Darcy Hunt also appeared as a witness since she was the first member of the police who questioned Cynthia. She told the following to the jury: *"I was there as a friend. Nancy called me, I arrived. I tell Cynthia she doesn't have to tell me anything. I was kind of aware of the situation before I got there. I basically explained to her that she's free to go at any time; she could fly to Jamaica if she wanted to. She basically confessed to what she had done and at that point, hours later when I leave, now I take the role of a police officer because now I have substantial evidence that she committed a murder.*" This testimony confirmed that Cynthia was not tricked to admit to murdering her boyfriend but that she did it willingly. The chances are she simply couldn't hide the secret anymore and needed to confess to someone.

While the initial toxicology report only proved that Thomas had antifreeze in his system, the second examination focused on the amount of the poisonous substance in his body after his death. Cynthia claimed that she wasn't sure about the amount of antifreeze she poured into the margarita container during her interview, suggesting that it might have been a single shot glass. However, Jeanne Beno who worked at Monroe County Medical Examiner's Office took the stand and revealed that Thomas Stack had consumed somewhere between 6 to 12 ounces of antifreeze which was way more than what Cynthia said. This testimony shook the defense's case to the core because it clearly wasn't an accident and Cynthia didn't want to only make him sick. The amount of Ethelyn glycol in that beverage suggested that she really did want to kill Thomas Stack.

Emily Galens, Cynthia's daughter who did confirm that her mother asked her to help her hide Thomas' body testified against Cynthia in the courtroom. The entire process was a very traumatic experience for this teenager, but she did her part properly, saying that as soon as her mother found Thomas Stack unconscious on the armchair, she called her down to the living room and asked if she could assist her with moving Thomas' body. It is important to mention that the man was still alive and breathing heavily. Emily said no and told her mother to call for help. The teenager refused to speak to the newspapers or any of the TV crews who were present at the courtroom.

Cynthia Galens did testify on her own behalf and everyone was waiting to hear her side of the story. She repeated that she didn't mean to poison her boyfriend and that his murder was a pure accident. The woman did confirm that life with Thomas Stack was difficult at times and that they argued often, mostly because of his excessive drinking and changing moods. He was very violent towards her at times and didn't hold back on threats against her daughter Emily. Cynthia saw herself as a devoted mother who only wanted to protect her child. The fact that she killed Thomas Stack by accident was a misfortune. Cynthia did have two police reports to back up her story. However, she did bail out Thomas both times, and the two got back together almost immediately. Cynthia also confirmed that no matter how much they fought, she loved Thomas and wanted to build a life with him.

The sentencing

The trial itself moved quickly and in the end, there was a total of twenty-three witnesses from both sides. The jury didn't deliberate for too long and they reached the verdict in only ninety minutes. She was now expecting a punishment of up to twenty-five years behind the bars. Cynthia's family was in obvious shock after the ruling. Her daughter Emily remained silent and refused to comment on the outcome. On the other hand, Cynthia's father Brad Stanton spoke with the news crew after the trial. He told them that his daughter was not a killer but she had to do the right thing in a given situation. Stanton also added the following: *"I know that Emily was horribly abused. Cindy lost her only son Matthew at age of nineteen. This man threatened to kill Emily."* Stanton also mentioned that he was glad his daughter was still alive and that Thomas Stack would have probably hurt her if he got a chance.

The prosecution was celebrating their victory, feeling that Thomas Stack finally got some justice. They were eager to hear how much time would Cynthia spend behind the bars. The lead prosecution told this to the news: *"It was a premeditated taking of another human life and I believe that it deserves the maximum sentence."* But a month would pass before Cynthia learns her destiny. Her father was hoping for a minimum sentence while the prosecution aimed at twenty-five years in prison.

On November 10th, 2010 Cynthia Galens appeared in front of a judge once again to find out which punishment she would receive for the first-degree murder of Thomas Stack. Judge William Kocher informed her that she would spend the next twenty-three years in prison. Cynthia appeared emotionless and showed no reaction to the sentencing. Thomas' mother Sandra was present in the courtroom and she told the media that the punishment was fair. The prosecution approved as well saying the following: *"There were a couple of things that were really important here. The fact that this was not a spur of the moment act but was premeditated, the fact that she had multiple opportunities to change course and do something to change his life and the fact that she lied to the doctors which ensured his death, I think all of those things militated toward a sentence approaching the maximum."*

The aftermath

Claiming that she received inadequate counsel from her attorney, Cynthia Galens filed an appeal to the Appellate Division of state Supreme Court. She hired a new attorney called Gary Muldoon who lived and worked in Rochester. Her defense attorney at the trial based the entire case around the fact that Cynthia killed her boyfriend accidentally and that she planned to poison him in order to run away from their abusive relationship. Unhappy with the outcome of her attorney's plan, she challenged the judge's initial decision wanting another trial. However, her appeal was denied by the court in November 2013.

The Appellate Division of state Supreme Court offered the following explanation: *"We note that defendant intentionally poured a large quantity of antifreeze into the victim's margarita mix and then, after knowing that the victim consumed the antifreeze, defendant failed to seek medical assistance for him despite seeing him foaming at the mouth and struggling to breathe. Under the circumstances, the sentence imposed by the county court, which is slightly less than the maximum sentence permitted by law, is appropriate."* The prosecution was happy with the rejected appeal, namely attorney R. Michael Tantillo who once again confirmed that the state did the right thing when they convicted

Cynthia of a first-degree murder. Cynthia remains locked up to this day, serving her sentence.

The Most Evil Woman Ever: THE TRUE STORY OF GERTRUDE BANISZEWSKI

OLIVIA WATSON

Chapter 1

There are few examples of pure evil more horrifying than the actions of Gertrude Baniszewski. In October, 1965, Indiana became home to one of the most cruel and horrifying murders the United States had ever seen—the murder of 16-year-old Sylvia Likens.

Sylvia and her sister Jenny were put into Baniszewski's care by their parents, whose work as carnies required them to travel frequently. They paid Baniszewski $20 a week for what they thought was room and board in a caring environment. The reality of Baniszewski's home was anything but.

Likens was tortured for three months by Baniszewski, Baniszewski's children, and their neighbourhood friends in a horrible game of emotional manipulation and terror. When Likens' will to live finally gave, her body followed. The 16-year-old finally passed away from shock, malnutrition, and a severe brain hemorrhage caused by months of severe beatings and other terrible deeds.

Gertrude Baniszewski was convicted of torturing and murdering the young girl in what the prosecutor described to be "the most terrible crime ever committed in the state of Indiana," the details of which continue to uphold that very reputation.

Chapter 2

Gertrude Baniszewski was born Gertrude Van Fossan to her parents, Hugh and Mollie Van Fossan, in Indianapolis, Indiana on September 19, 1929. She was the third of six children. The young girl had an average childhood for the time, but this happy childhood came to an abrupt end in 1939 when Gertrude's father passed away suddenly from a heart attack in front of her own eyes.

After the death of Hugh, the Van Fossan family fell into hardship. Mollie, Gertrude's now-widowed mother, had six children to support on her own and little prospects. Gertrude was forced to leave school when she was only sixteen. Her mother needed help supporting her siblings, so Gertrude began looking for a job.

Gertrude quickly found a job at a local pharmacy working as a saleswoman. Although she didn't enjoy working, she disliked seeing her earnings leave her possession as soon as she received them. Almost all of her paychecks went directly to her financially failing family.

Gertrude resented her mother for forcing her to abandon her education in favour of working, and even more for taking her earnings. The pretty, young girl felt like she was destined for things greater than her poverty-stricken lifestyle allowed for. When she was out in the world working, she enjoyed meeting new people, especially men with an eye for young beauties, and the separation it gave her from her family.

High off her newly found independence, Gertrude left her family for good, the same year she left school, to marry John Baniszewski, an 18-year-old suburban police officer. Gertrude and John's relationship lasted over ten years, but it was no respite from the poverty she was hoping to leave behind.

Together, the couple had four children: Paul, Stephanie, John, and Marie. Gertrude stopped working in order to raise the children, and the family scraped by on John's basic salaries. John had a volatile temper and was verbally abusive to his children. He was also physically abusive to Gertrude throughout the entire marriage.

Again craving her freedom, Gertrude sought ways to leave her husband, but was unable to find a solution she could monetarily support until 1955, when John was stationed outside of Indiana for training. Claiming she was unable to bear the stress or financial strain of moving the family, Gertrude Baniszewski left her husband and filed for divorce.

Those around Gertrude, including her children, hoped that this would be a new start for Baniszewski and her four children. However, the drama that would continue to plague the rest of their time together as a family was just starting to begin.

Within months of divorcing her husband, Gertrude Baniszewski had moved in with a new boyfriend, remarried, divorced, and returned to Indiana where she reunited with John Baniszewski, who had since returned from his temporary posting. Together, the couple had two more children, Marie and Shirley, but never remarried.

Gertrude and John Baniszewski parted ways again after the birth of their sixth child together, this time for good. John's abuses had gotten more physical and was directed more towards the children as his temper became shorter and more volatile. Gertrude was left alone now with six children to support. Many expected Gertrude to settle down and find a job, but the 34-year-old woman wasn't done searching for romance. She always seemed to think of her needs first, and her next move shocked many.

In 1963, Baniszewski found a new lover: 18-year-old Dennis Lee Wright. While the couple claimed to be happy together, they never married, and the signs of physical abuse were obvious on both Baniszewski and her six children. While the pair was never married, Baniszewski and Wright had a son together, and they named him after his father, Dennis Lee Wright Jr.

Shortly after the birth of their child, Dennis Lee Wright walked out of his and Baniszewski's home never to return. Baniszewski was left alone with her seven children, all of whom were crammed into the family's small two bedroom home. The children shared the bedrooms and set up camp in the living room, but the couch was reserved for Gertrude.

With a newborn baby and no money for childcare, Gertrude Baniszewski was forced to be a stay-at-home mother. She took up work from home ironing clothes to help make ends meet, but the majority of the family's small income came from welfare. Along with Baniszewski and her seven children, the house was also full of neighbourhood kids. The rundown, dirty house was a popular hangout spot as the children could be messy as they liked and could come and go as they pleased, no questions asked.

Two friends of the Baniszewski children were Jenny and Sylvia Likens. The Baniszewski's met the two girls in their neighbourhood. They got along famously, and Jenny and Sylvia were invited to stay the night. It was the beginning of a friendship none of them would ever forget.

Chapter 3

Sylvia and Jenny Likens were close sisters. Sylvia had been born between two sets of twins, one of which Jenny belonged to, but Jenny and Sylvia were much closer than Jenny and her fraternal sibling. The two spent all their time together and often had the same friends. Both girls enjoyed spending time at the Baniszewski household.

Although the girls shared much in common, they were different in many ways as well. Jenny was a Polio victim; she was often weak and timid. Jenny liked to blend into the crowd and hardly spoke up for herself.

Sylvia was Jenny's voice. Sylvia was spunky. She was outgoing, loud, and was proud of her good looks. She enjoyed being the center of attention, but was never rude. She was a caring person who always looked after her ailing younger sister. Jenny's needs always came before Sylvia.

In 1965, the Likens family was going through a tough time. Jenny and Sylvia's parents had recently separated and the girls moved in with their mother, Betty. Before they separated, both Betty and the girls' father, Lester, were carnival workers. While they didn't make a lot of money, they made enough to get by. But the job also came with frequent travel requirements, so the family's children often had to stay apart with relatives or miss school. Betty wanted to change this.

When Betty left her husband and took her daughters with her, she had a hard time finding new employment. Working as a carnie left her with few transferrable skills, and times were tough. Eventually, Betty turned to crime to support her family and was caught shoplifting, a crime she was put in jail for.

When Betty Likens was arrested and jailed for shoplifting, Jenny and Sylvia were put back into the care of their father, Lester Likens. Lester was unable to give up his job as a carnival worker, understanding he had few other prospects to lean on for money. He was also unable to afford to move his children around with him. He began to look for alternative housing arrangements for his children.

Lester wanted his girls to be able to stay in their hometown of Indianapolis so they could continue to attend the same school as before, but the family didn't have any relatives in the area for the girls to stay with so Lester got creative.

Lester Likens knew his daughters had been welcomed at the Baniszewski household and that Gertrude was a single mother of seven. Surely, she loved having a full household and needed some extra cash. The night before he left town with his carnival company, Lester paid Gertrude Baniszewski a visit.

Gertrude Baniszewski was initially unreceptive of having the two Likens girls staying in her house—it was rundown and overcrowded already. However, her tune quickly changed when Lester said he was willing to pay for the girls room and board. Desperate to have some extra cash, Baniszewski agreed to house, feed, and care for the two girls for $20 a week. Lester would be back in four months to collect the girls.

Initially, $20 a week sounded like a great deal to Baniszewski, but when she was left with the girls she quickly remembered that $20 for two girls would hardly be enough to cover the cost of food, let alone anything else. She quickly began to resent the extra responsibility the two girls presented, even though she had agreed to take it on.

While Lester later admitted he intentionally avoided looking into the condition of the household he was leaving his two daughters in, he had no way of knowing just what his daughters would endure over the course of the next few months. Gertrude Baniszewski was the last person anyone should have left their children with.

Baniszewski was was cold and distant, and she gave the impression that she wasn't exactly all there. In reality, Baniszewski was depressed, she was worn out. Baniszewski's health had been in a steep decline recently; she was chronically ill with a number of unidentified illnesses, ceased practicing proper hygiene, and barely ate; eventually, these factors began to affect her outward appearance, resulting in a receded hairline, sunken eyes, and an overall skeletal appearance.

The home was no better. Besides lacking enough beds for half the people in the house, it also had no stove or microwave; the only things Gertrude kept in her pantry were bread and crackers; most of the surfaces in the home were caked with thick layers of dirt; and the family only had enough plates and eating utensils for three people. It was hell.

Chapter 4

The first week of Sylvia and Jenny's visit went surprisingly well. The two girls attended school with the Baniszewski children and were invited to attend church and other social events with them as well. This quickly changed, however, when Lester's second payment was late.

When Lester's first payment was late in the mail, Baniszewski was furious. She snapped. Enraged that she may have just been duped into caring for the girls for free, she decided that she would receive payment another way—throught the enjoyment of seeing the young girls in pain.

Baniszewski forced the two girls to bend over on the kitchen table with their skirts up and underwear down. She then beat both of the girls' buttocks with a wooden paddle. If the physical pain wasn't enough for the girls to bear, Baniszewski also insisted on having her children watch. *This is what happens when you cross me* was the lesson she wanted them to all learn.

This first instance of abuse was directed at both of the Likens girls, but it would be only one of the few Jenny would be forced to endure.

Baniszewski quickly focused her hatred towards Sylvia, who, at the age of sixteen, reminded Baniszewski of everything she had had to give up at the same age—her education, her beauty, and her youth. She was the embodiment, and now seemingly a cause, of everything Gertrude had lost at the hands of poverty.

Sylvia also sacrificed herself frequently to save her sister from Baniszewski's torture. Sylvia and Jenny once collected bottles for days to save up some change for candy. When Baniszewski saw the treat, she accused the girls of stealing. It was Sylvia who stood up to Gertrude and told her how they had gotten the candy, so it was Sylvia who received the beating. The cycle had already begun.

Early on, Sylvia and Jenny believed that spanking was the worst Gertrude could do to them, and Sylvia could grin and bear a beating for the sake of some candy and her sister. It quickly became apparent that Baniszewski was capable of much worse though. One Sunday afternoon the Baniszewski children attended a church social with Sylvia and Jenny, which included a meal. Jenny and Sylvia had been barely fed since staying with the Baniszewski's, something they were not used to yet, so they went back for seconds, and in Sylvia's case, thirds.

When the children returned home, the Baniszewski's told their mother of how Sylvia had eaten so much. Gertrude was infuriated at what she saw as Sylvia's attempt to ruin her own physical appearance, so she forced the girl to eat a hot dog that was piled high with condiments. When she vomited, she was then forced to eat it as well. It was only two weeks into her stay with the Baniszewski's, but Sylvia's nightmare had already begun.

Chapter 5

Gertrude Baniszewski had not been well for years; she was asthmatic, depressed, and worn out. But her mental state took a severe decline under the stress of having two extra children to feed and care for. It only took one small incident for Gertrude to snap permanently into a sadist decline, and after this small incident Gertrude's treatment of Sylvia went from abuse to full-blown torture.

One afternoon Sylvia was in the family's living room chatting to one of Gertrude's daughters about an experience she had had with a boy a few months before she came to live with the Baniszewski's. Sylvia had been dating the boy for several weeks and had let him feel her up. Gertrude Baniszewski overheard the story and flew into a fit of rage, accusing Sylvia of being a prostitute, and telling the rest of the household that Sylvia was pregnant because she had let a boy touch her crotch.

Gertrude then attacked Sylvia, repeatedly kicking her in the crotch. When the beating was over, Sylvia attempted to sit in a chair to calm down, but Gertrude Baniszewski wouldn't let her. Sylvia was told she didn't deserve to sit in her charis, and was now only allowed to do so with permission.

From this point onwards in the Baniszewski household, Sylvia was nothing but a plaything. Everything that went wrong in the family was blamed on Sylvia, and the Baniszewski children were encouraged to use her for games, which ranged from beating the girl, tying her up, and pushing her down the stairs. Sylvia also became the household ashtray, any Baniszewski who smoked began arbitrarily extinguishing their cigarettes on her skin. Gertrude also began to deliver bizarre sermons to her children, justifying their acts as proper treatment for prostitutes.

The Baniszewski children were not the only ones to be encouraged to join in on the torture of Sylvia though. Gertrude convinced several friends of her children that Sylvia was spreading nasty rumors about them around town. She invited her daughter Stephanie's boyfriend, Coy Hubbard, to the home several times and encouraged him to practice his Judo on Sylvia as punishment for Sylvia spreading a rumor that Stephanie had sex for money. She also convinced Sylvia's own best friend, Anna Sisco, that Sylvia had called her mother a whore. She brought Sisco to the house to confront Sylvia and encouraged the girls to fist fight each other.

In another attempt to remove all friendship and love from Sylvia's life, Gertrude forced Sylvia's sister Jenny to physically attack her. Jenny had initially refused until Gertrude began beating her, something Jenny could not withstand in her weakened state. Jenny eventually had to give in and punch her sister until Gertrude told her she could stop.

While all this was happening, Sylvia continued to go to school with Jenny and the rest of the Baniszewski children. School was the only break Sylvia got from Baniszewski's abuse, although she had become withdrawn and was often confronted by her torturess peers on the schoolyard. Sylvia never told any adults about the abuse, likely because Gertrude threatened to harm or kill Jenny if she did.

Sylvia still enjoyed school though, but she started getting in trouble for not showing up to gym class with the proper attire. She was required to wear a sweat suit to participate, but Gertrude refused to buy her one. Sylvia didn't want to get into any more trouble so she stole a change of clothes from a classmate. Gertrude quickly caught on to the fact that Sylvia had stolen and eventually got Sylvia to confess to the crime. For this, Sylvia was removed from her school by Gertrude, but that wasn't the only punishment she would receive.

Gertrude believed that she was right about Sylvia being a thief, so she had to be right about her being a prostitute as well. So she told Sylvia she was going to show her what it was like to be a prostitute.

Gertrude gathered all of her sons, and some of the boys from around the neighbourhood, into one room with Sylvia. She then made the 16-year-old strip and masturbate with a glass Coca Cola bottle, threatening to beat Jenny if she refused. To protect her sister, Sylvia complied with Gertrude's horrific demands. It was the beginning of the end for Sylvia.

Chapter 6

After the cola bottle incident, Sylvia's body began to give out. It was bruised, battered, and covered in cigarette burns. She became incontinent, so Gertrude moved the girl to the basement, where she was locked in and forced to urinate and defecate on the floor.

Sylvia was living in filth against her own will, and was begging to be able to bathe, so Gertrude came up with a solution that fit her own needs to abuse the girl. She established a cleansing routine for Sylvia, which involved filling the family bathtub with hot water, binding Sylvia's limbs together, and submerging the helpless girl into the scalding water. The regime was administered arbitrarily; Sylvia would be bathed in this way sometimes once a day, sometimes several times a day, and sometimes not at all. Following baths, the Baniszewski's would rub handfuls of salt over Sylvia's nude, burned body.

After a few weeks of living in the basement, Gertrude made Sylvia a deal. She brought her upstairs and tied her up to one of the family's few beds. Gertrude told the young girl that if she could go the whole night without wetting the bed, she could again live amongst the family. Sylvia was left tied to the bed for over nine hours, making it impossible for her to comply to Gertrude's demands. When Gertrude found she had wet the bed the next day, she lashed out at the girl and forced her to perform another strip tease and cola bottle sex show for her sons.

At this point, Gertrude was completely out of control. Throughout the whole second cola bottle incident, the boys who were watching shouted at Sylvia that she was a prostitute, and she was proud of it. Sylvia tried to cry, but her body was so dehydrated she was physically unable to. Gertrude was so pleased with the incident that she decided Sylvia should remember it for the rest of her life.

After the incident was over, Gertrude got the boys to carry Sylvia to one of the bedrooms and tie her up, still naked, to a bed. She then grabbed a sewing needle, which she heated in the flame of a candle, and used the needle to carve the boys' phrase into Sylvia's abdomen. I'm a prostitute, and proud of it.

That night, Sylvia was again forced to sleep naked in the basement. Jenny was allowed to pay her sister a visit, during which time Sylvia told Jenny that she could feel her body giving out. She was sure she was going to die.

When she went back upstairs, Jenny told Gertrude that Sylvia thought she was dying in an attempt to lighten the abuse. Instead, it made Gertrude realize that Sylvia's death was a real possibility and she needed a plan just in case.

In the morning, Gertrude sat down with Sylvia and forced her to write a letter to her parents stating that she had left the Baniszewski house to run away with a gang of boys. She forced Sylvia to write how these imagined boys continuously raped and beat her, even burning her with their cigarettes and carving the terrible tattoo into her skin. Gertrude wanted an excuse for every blemish in the young girl's skin.

Baniszewski later told police that her final plan for Sylvia was to have her write this letter, which would be mailed to her parents, and then to leave her in a nearby garbage dump to die. Sylvia apparently heard Gertrude telling this to her children, and began to rebel against her abuser for the first time.

On her last day alive, Sylvia was offered both toast and crackers to eat, the first real food the young girl had seen in over a week, but Sylvia refused to eat it. As punishment, Gertrude tried to beat Sylvia with a chair, but Sylvia dodged the attack and the chair broke against a wall. Gertrude then tried to beat Sylvia with a paddle, but Sylvia again dodged the attack and Gertrude ended up hitting her own face, blacking her eye. Gertrude then called down her son John, who beat Sylvia unconscious with a broom.

These small acts of defiance would be Sylvia's last acts alive.

Chapter 7

On October 26, 1965, the morning after Sylvia defied Gertrude Baniszewski for the first time, the Baniszewski children were instructed by Gertrude to go and bathe the young girl they had been keeping captive in the basement. The children complied, it was something they did on a regular basis. But something was different this morning; when the children tied Sylvia's limbs up and dropped her into the scalding hot water, she didn't scream.

The children removed her from the tub and noticed she wasn't breathing. Frightened, Stephanie Baniszewski began to try and give Sylvia mouth-to-mouth resuscitation, but it was far too late. Sylvia had died in her sleep sometime the night before. She had died before allowing Gertrude Baniszewski to carry out her final plans, and with that final act of defiance, Sylvia's living hell had finally come to an end.

Sylvia's body was taken downstairs and stripped, and the police were called from a neighbour's house. Initially, Gertrude was not worried about the police finding out about Sylvia's death. She had Sylvia's handwritten note, and her children were either part of the crime or too afraid to speak out against her. Or so she thought.

During the police's examination of the rundown house, Jenny Likens silently snuck up to one of the officers and whispered into his ear that if he got her out of that place, she would tell him exactly what had happened to her sister. The officer complied.

When Jenny told the story of how her sister had died, the police were shocked, but they were quickly able to find a mountain of evidence to corroborate her terrible tale. Sylvia's body was emancipated to a state that the coroner described as being consistent with a holocaust victim. She had over 100 cigarette burns on her skin. Her official cause of death was shock and severe brain hemorrhaging, which was caused by the prolonged and horrific abuse her body endured.

Gertrude Baniszewski was tried and quickly convicted of first-degree murder, despite her claims that she had not taken part in the abuse, and that she had been too concerned to control what her children did.

Two of the Baniszewski children, Paula and John, as well as two of their friends were also tried for their part in Sylvia's torture. Paula was convicted of second-degree murder, while John and their friends were convicted of manslaughter.

After Gertrude Baniszewski was arrested, Jenny Likens was reunited with both her father and mother, who were horrified at the way they lost Sylvia, but grateful that one of their children had survived the atrocious actions of the woman they trusted to care for their daughters.

While Sylvia was finally free from all harm, the story of how she came to die will never be forgotten by her family, her friends, and all who knew the beautiful, warm, and loving young girl.

TEEN KILLER: THE TRUE STORY OF ERIN CAFFEY

AMY DELANEY

Erin Caffey

The clock on the wall of the Caffey house showed 3.55am – the time that the flames had engulfed the Texan cabin which had been home to Terry Caffey, 41, his 37-year-old wife, Penny, and their three children – 16-year-old Erin, Matthew, 13, and Tyler, who was 8.

But it wasn't the fire which had claimed the lives of Terry's family.

Erin's Childhood

Terry Caffey's life revolved around the Baptist faith, and it was at one of the church's meetings, when he was 24, that his attention was caught by 21-year-old Penny Lynn Daily – the pretty blond who played the piano for the church. Terry was captivated by her – not only by her beauty but by her welcoming smile and her ability to give her undivided attention to whoever she was speaking to.

"Basically, she had me at 'hello."

The pair became quickly inseparable, and they were married within eight months. A year later, on July 27th, 1991, their first child, Erin, was born.

Terry was overcome with love for his newborn daughter, as he held her in his arms.

"I made a promise that I would stand by her. I didn't say, 'I'll stand by you if you're a good girl,' or 'I'll stand by you if you do what I say.' I told her I'd stand by her."[1]

Little did the proud, doting father know how far that pledge would be tested just 16 years later.

In 1994, Matthew Ryan was born, and five years later Tyler Paul completed the family.[2]

Up until the age of 12 or 13, Erin lived with her parents and two younger brothers in Point, Texas, where Erin attended school in the nearby town of Celeste.

The family were devout Baptists and decided to move to Alba when Erin was 13 to be nearer to the church where both Terry and Penny worked – The Miracle Faith Baptist Church. As well as being a delivery driver for a home health company, Terry was following his dream of becoming an ordained minister with the church, and regularly gave sermons there.

Indeed, the whole Caffey family was involved with the faith. Penny played the piano for the church and was also a member of the gospel singing group – The Gaston Singers – who performed at churches in the area. When she wasn't singing or playing with the church, she would deliver meals to elderly people, or those who couldn't afford to eat.

13-year-old Matthew, who was affectionately known as Bubba, was an accomplished musician, playing both the bass guitar and harmonica at the church, and 8-year-old Tyler would often accompany him.

Erin, the oldest child and only daughter, would sing in church – sometimes alongside her mother but often she would sing solo. She had a beautiful voice, and the local parishioners loved to hear her perform.[3]

Homeschooling

Only a month into the eighth grade at her new school, Penny and Terry Caffey withdrew their children from public school and started homeschooling them, using a bible based curriculum. Their reason for doing so was that another girl at the school had tried to kiss Erin.

The issue of bisexuality was a huge concern to the Caffey's – so much so, in fact, that this incident was later blamed for Erin's subsequent catastrophic behaviour, with Terry saying that the kiss confused his daughter *"before she finally veered off into the premarital relationship that turned deadly."*[4]

Homeschooling was, to all intents and purposes, an isolating experience for Erin and her brothers. Their home was one of three houses which shared more than 100 acres of land and was six miles from town, so company was sparse outside of the family and church.

The Caffey family's life revolved around religious studies and pastimes, leaving little time for other activities. Sundays were given over to church services, and Wednesday evenings were for bible study. On Saturdays, Penny would cook a meal to bring to church the next day, and in between these sessions, the children would practice their gospel readings. Family Bible time would also take place frequently, during which the family would discuss the Scriptures.[5]

The heavy church-related workload, and the isolated location of the family home did not leave much room for play or friendships – something which the previously sociable Erin must have found strange.

Young Love

In 2007, when Erin was 16, her parents allowed her to take a job at the Sonic, a local drive-in fast food restaurant. Erin was a pretty girl and the only waitress there who delivered her orders on roller skates. She frequently attracted the attention of boys – so much so that they would check out which side of the car park Erin was serving to ensure she delivered their food.[6]

However, she was not worldly wise – as one of her co-workers put it *"She was so sheltered. It was like she was seeing the world for the first time."*[7]

Another said when interviewed *"She gushed innocence. A lot of guys flirted with her, and she would just blush and smile and duck her head down and skate inside and tell me, 'That guy wanted my number!' And I'd say, 'Did you tell him that your mom would be answering the phone?'"[8]*

One young man, did, however, catch Erin's eye.

In the summer of 2007, 19-year-old Charlie Wilkinson drove his 1991 Ford Explorer into the Sonic, where he saw Erin for the first time. As Erin rolled up to his car on her roller skates to deliver his order, Charlie felt an instant connection, and from that moment on he was smitten.

Although he was known for being easily wound up, Charlie Wilkinson had never been in trouble with the police and had no disciplinary problems at school. Friends would deliberately aggravate him, but, although he would sometimes lash out at his desk, or storm out of the room, Charlie would always walk away from a fight.

He lived with his father and step-mother in the country, along with his step-brother and step-sister, and a half-sister. Much of his time was spent hunting and fishing, and – like most of his peers – he knew how to handle a gun.

It took Charlie several visits to the Sonic before he plucked up the courage to ask Erin out on a date, but once he did, shortly after Halloween 2007, the pair became infatuated with each other.

According to a friend of Charlie's, Dion Kipp Jr, *"He was totally in love with her and considered her his soul mate...Charlie talked about Erin twenty-four-seven."*

It was an infatuation which was to have fatal consequences.

Erin invited Charlie home to meet her parents, but the meeting did not leave a good impression on Terry, who had arrived home from work to find the teenager sitting with his leg hanging over the side of Terry's armchair. To make matters worse, when Terry said hello, Charlie did not stand up or even shake the older man's hand.

He told his wife, Penny *"I don't like that boy...if he can't show me any respect, how does he treat our daughter?"*

The Caffeys allowed the pair to date, although forbade them from spending time together away from the family home. Every afternoon, he and Erin would spend her lunch break at the Sonic together, and Charlie would spend the evenings with Erin at the house. Terry and Penny made sure that Charlie left by 9 o clock, but even that was not the end of the young couple's contact for the day – Erin would call Charlie on the phone after he left, and their conversations would continue until her 10 pm curfew.

In order to spend even more time with his girl, Charlie also started going to Miracle Faith and attending services there. Pastor McGahee remembers:

"What I knew of Charlie, he seemed like a nice boy, I don't think anyone worried about him and Erin at first. We thought it was just puppy love."

However, people soon began to take notice of the young couple, for all the wrong reasons. Children from the congregation saw them kissing at a table behind the church, with Charlie slipping his hand under Erin's shirt. When the new youth director caught them, Penny and Terry were mortified and separated the couple. Embarrassed by their daughter's behaviour, they told Erin that she was no longer allowed to see Charlie.[8]

Pastor's wife, Rebecca McGahee later said *"That's not the girl we knew, it's just not...we had all talked to her about this boyfriend and told her, 'Don't get swindled into something you're not ready for.' But we were thinking sex; we weren't thinking murder."*

Penny and Terry shared their concerns with their friends at the church about Charlie's possessiveness and drinking. However, whenever the subject was broached with Erin, her reply was always the same.

"I know. I'm confused. I want to please my parents, but I like him."[9]

In December 2007, Erin told her parents that she wanted to return to school. By that time it was only Erin who was being home schooled

– her two brothers had already returned as Matthew had started to miss his friends, so Erin was even more isolated at home. Penny wanted the opportunity to earn extra money, and Erin going back to school would free up her time to work more hours, so they agreed, and Erin returned to public school just before Christmas 2007.

Freshman Erin was able to spend more time with Charlie at school, and they would spend every lunchtime together and would be seen holding hands as they walked to classes together, or would disappear to Erin's truck to make out.

Penny and Terry decided to lift their restrictions slightly and allowed Charlie to take Erin out to dinner occasionally, on the proviso that he had their daughter home by 9.30pm.

It was during one of these outings that 16-year-old Erin had sex with Charlie for the first time.

The Engagement

A few days later, while at a church meeting, Penny noticed a ring on her daughter's finger. Charlie had taken Erin out, and, after pulling over on a country road, had gotten down on one knee and presented Erin with his Grandmother's engagement ring. Although he had not asked Erin to marry him, saying it was a 'promise' ring rather than an engagement ring, his intentions were clear.

Penny was furious and told Erin she had to return the ring to Charlie. Terry decided to have it out with Charlie and confronted him during a basketball game outside the church. He took Charlie to one side and tried to reason with him.

"This is totally inappropriate...you're promising yourself to my daughter? Do you realize she is sixteen years old?"

Charlie remained unmoved and shrugged at Terry's words.

The Caffeys decided to severely limit the young couple's time together, allowing them to see each other only once a week. This enraged Erin, who began to hatch a plot to run away with Charlie when she turned 17.

Things went from bad to worse at the Caffey house, and there were frequent arguments between Erin and her mother. One night, Erin called Charlie, crying, saying that her mother had hit her. Charlie reported Penny to the police, claiming that Erin felt that she was in danger at her mother's hand.

Friends at Miracle Faith began to notice that things were amiss with the Caffey family. Throughout February of 2008 Penny became more and more withdrawn, and even turned down the opportunity to go on a women's retreat with the church. Her reasons, when pressed, were that she needed to concentrate on her family. Erin continued to attend functions at the church, but had become aloof and would not participate. She appeared to be distracted, so much so that, at a Valentine's Day dinner at her youth club, the normally helpful and diligent Erin wouldn't even fill glasses with water.

It was during February that Penny overheard Erin giggling one night in her room. She had sneaked her cell phone into her room past her curfew and was talking and laughing with Charlie.

Penny had had enough and grounded Erin. Not only that, but she also took her daughter's car keys and cell phone, and revoked Charlie's weekly visits. Terry and Penny drove Erin to and from school every day, so opportunities to see Charlie were severely limited.

On February 21st, Terry's father died of a heart attack. The family had never been particularly close, but, to honour him, the Caffeys performed *Amazing Grace* at his funeral. The whole family took part, with Penny playing the piano while Terry and Matthew played the harmonica. The congregation, who always loved it when Erin sang, were taken aback, however, when her performance was flat and listless.

Rebecca McGahee, the pastor's wife, was particularly troubled by the change in Erin.

"Erin's anointing had lifted...she couldn't sing a lick."

The Plot

The reason for Erin's distraction was simple – at her grandfather's funeral, she was already plotting her family's murder.

She began obsessing about murdering her parents, telling Charlie it was the only way they could be together. She wasn't discreet about it – in the middle of February, a junior at school overheard Erin discussing it with Charlie.

Charlie told several of his friends that he intended killing the Caffeys, but admitted that all he really wanted to do was run away with Erin. Charlie's father said that he had a compulsion to rescue people – he called it 'lost puppy dog syndrome' – and that that's what he wanted to do with Erin...rescue her.

He even hatched his own plot to get Erin pregnant so that her parents would have no choice about letting them be together, but Erin refused, telling Charlie she was too young for a baby, reminding him again that they would never be together while her parents were alive. Contrary to what her parents thought, it was, in actual fact, Erin who was in control of Charlie and not the other way around. A senior at the school said:

"She had him around her finger, pretty much...she could get him to do whatever she wanted. She asked for something, she got it."

The final straw for Erin came on February 27th, after Penny had visited the local library to check up on Charlie's MySpace online profile, at her sister's suggestion – the same sister to whom Erin had told her plans of running away with Charlie when she turned 17.

Penny was horrified to read Charlie's comments about drinking and having sex and told Terry what she had discovered. When Erin arrived home later that day, her parents were waiting for her.

Ready for another argument, Terry told Erin that it was over between her and Charlie and that she was not to see him again, but instead of shouting and crying, Erin agreed. Furthermore, she told her parents that she had been trying to end the relationship with Charlie for some time, but hadn't been able to find a reason to. She promised her parents that she would end things with her boyfriend.

The Murders

On the night of February 29th, 2008, Charlie Wilkinson received a call from Erin. Her assurances to her parents that she would end her relationship were nothing more than a ruse to placate them, and she was angry at their insistence that she no longer see her boyfriend. Charlie told Erin that they should just run away together, but she was adamant that she wanted them dead, replying *"No, kill them."*

In the early hours of the following morning, at around 1.30am, Charlie and his friend, 20-year-old Charles Waid, drove to the Caffey's home with Bobbi Johnson, Waid's 18-year-old girlfriend. Charles Waid needed money, and Charlie had promised him $2000 if he helped him kill the Caffeys. The money, Erin told Charlie, could be found in a box inside the Caffey house. Their first attempt was thwarted by the Caffey's dog barking, and they drove away.

Erin called Charlie and told him to come back, saying she would keep the dog quiet, so Charlie, Charles, and Bobbi returned to the house.

Erin was waiting for them at the end of the driveway, and they drove away to discuss their plan. Charlie asked Erin several times to just run away with him, but she insisted that she wanted her parents dead.

They returned, and parked Bobbi's silver Dodge a little way from the house, with Erin's plan firmly embedded in their minds. Charlie was to murder Penny and Terry, while Waid, a father himself, took care of Erin's two younger brothers to ensure there were no witnesses.

Erin wanted her entire family slaughtered.

According to Charlie, the two men entered the Caffey's house through the open front door, while Erin and Bobbi waited in the car.

Their first victims were Penny and Terry. The men entered their ground floor bedroom with a .22 caliber pistol and a couple of samurai swords. Charlie opened fire on the couple but his gun jammed after several shots. Waid took the pistol and fixed it before shooting at the couple again. The men left the room, but, to make sure Penny was dead, Charlie returned and slashed her throat with a sword, almost decapitating her.

Sure that the adults were dead, Waid told Charlie that it was the boys' turn.

"Little ones talk."

Charlie didn't want to hurt the boys, but when Waid threatened to leave, Charlie called to the boys, who had locked themselves in Erin's room, to get back into their own beds. When Matthew tried to resist, Waid raised the gun and shot the 13-year-old in the face. Matthew fell and didn't move again. Waid then turned his attention to the youngest boy, Tyler, who he stabbed to death.

Certain that the family was deceased, Charlie carried a pre-packed suitcase containing some of Erin's belongings, out to the car before the two men returned to the house to take what they could find. Their final act of destruction, before driving away, was to set fire to the house.[10]

Terry

However, unknown to the murderers, not everyone died in the massacre. Terry, having been shot multiple times, had passed out, giving the appearance of being dead. When he came to, the men were gone and he discovered his wife with her throat slashed. The fire was consuming the upper floor where his children slept, but he was unable to reach them because the flames were too strong. The right side of his body was numb, and the only choice he had was to escape himself and raise the alarm.

Once through the bathroom window, Terry began a laborious journey to his neighbours' home. Terry had no idea whether the attackers were still on the grounds, but what he did know was that one of them was his daughter's boyfriend, Charlie Wilkinson.

Bleeding heavily, it took Terry over an hour to get to Tommy and Helen Gaston's house, crawling through the wooded grounds and falling into a creek on the way, but finally, he made it.

Tommy discovered Terry, bleeding, wet and muddy on his doorstep. He asked Terry where Penny and the children were, and all Terry could answer was *"They're all dead".*

When firefighters eventually put out the fire, they discovered Penny's body in the doorway of the bedroom she shared with her husband. Beneath her body, they found three .22 caliber casings. Matthews's body was found in the living room, and Tyler was found on what remained of his parents' bed, among items of Erin's clothing. The second floor had collapsed in the fire, bringing the boys crashing through the ceiling onto the floor below. It appeared that Tyler had been hiding in Erin's closet, among her clothes, when he was stabbed to death.

What puzzled police the most was that they were unable to locate Erin's body.

The Arrest

Terry told police that he believed Charlie Wilkinson had been responsible for the murders. He had heard his sons and his wife calling out Charlie's name in fear before he blacked out. While doctors worked to remove the bullets from Terry's head and back, police arrested Charlie Wilkinson.[11]

When police searched Charlie's trailer, they found Erin hiding under a pile of clothes, among piles of trash. When questioned, she told the police that two men dressed all in black had forced their way into her bedroom and made her drink something, after which, she claimed, she had passed out. However, at the hospital toxicology reports showed that no drugs or other suspicious substances had been consumed. She remembered there being flames – however, none of Erin's clothes actually smelt of smoke.

While Erin was at the hospital, Charlie Wilkinson, Charles Waid and Bobbi Johnson were being interviewed by Sergeant John Vance and Detective Richard Almon. All three of the suspects' stories concurred – that, despite being urged to the contrary, Erin had insisted that her family be murdered.

Furthermore, according to detective Almon, Erin had said *"You'll have to kill the older one because he'll talk. And go ahead and kill the younger one because he's a brat and I don't like him anyway."*

At this time, Erin was being taken to the East Texas Medical Center to visit her father, after being told he had survived the attack. Detective Almon had the vehicle carrying Erin stopped, and her grandmother, Virginia Daily, who was travelling with her, was told that Erin was under suspicion of murder.

"They told me she had been implicated in the murders...and I looked that child in the eye and asked her if she had anything to do with it, and she said, 'No, Grandma.'"[12]

When Terry Caffey was told by his sister, Mary, that his daughter had been found alive and well, he was overjoyed. His joy was short-lived, however, when a few minutes later he was informed that his 16-year-old daughter had been charged with the murders of his wife and two little boys.

"I screamed and tried to rip the drips out of my arms. I was crying and shouting: 'No, not Erin.' It was unthinkable she'd been involved."[13]

The Trials

In November 2008 Charlie Wilkinson, 19, and Charles Waid, 20, pled guilty to capital murder, and both were sentenced to life in prison without parole.[14]

At their hearing, Terry spoke to both the men. Waid showed no remorse or emotion, but Charlie was tearful.

"In time, God has shown me what it means to forgive...Charlie Wilkinson, I want to say to you today, I forgive you. Not so much for your sake, but for my own. I refuse to grow into a bitter old man. If I want to

heal and move on, I must find some forgiveness in my heart, and that has been the hardest thing I have ever had to do because you took so much from me."[15]

Two months later, on January 2nd, 2009, Bobbi Johnson pled guilty to being an accomplice and was sentenced to 40 years in prison, with the possibility of parole after 20 years.[16]

On the same date, Erin Caffey, by then 17 and determined as an adult to stand trial, agreed to a plea bargain, following all three of her accomplices naming her as the mastermind behind the massacre. She received two life sentences for the murders of her brothers, Matthew and Tyler, with a further 25 years for her mother's murder. She will be eligible for parole when she reaches the age of 59.

Despite the fact that his daughter brought about the brutal deaths of his wife and sons, Terry Caffey still visits his daughter in prison, and his biggest wish is that he lives long enough to see his daughter released.

"Erin will be 59 by the time she's eligible for parole and I'll be 86. I pray I can have a few years with her. I know people will find it hard to understand my forgiveness, but she's my daughter and I'll always love her, no matter what"[17]

But, according to Rains County Attorney Robert Vititow, Terry might never get his wish.

"As for Erin Caffey, two life sentences, will she ever parole out? I can't answer that. And if she did, she would still have another 25-year sentence to serve and so the odds are that she may never get out."[18]

A MURDER FOREVER UNSOLVED

SAMANTHA REED

Beulah Louise Overell: An Explosive Cover-up

Murder is an age-old thing. Many people believe that crime and violence is a new phenomenon, but people have been killing each other for various reasons for all of recorded history. So it is no surprise that when we look back a few decades we can still find some rather interesting murder cases. People murder for love, money, vengeance, personal advancement, or simply for the fun of it. This case, out of Orange Country, California is no exception to those motivations. And even seventy years after the fact, these murders still remain quite exceptional.

Due to the age of the case the case files are scarce and much of what actually happened is mere journalistic speculation. Much of what is said about what happened has been exaggerated or assumed. So take it all with a grain of salt as we seek to find the facts within the years of fiction.

The Happy Couple

The year was 1947. The United States of America was just seeing the end of the Second World War. Soldiers were returning home. Families were beginning to rebuild. The country itself was going to enter into one of its most prosperous periods. And yet, things were not all happy families and white picket fences.

Beulah Louise Overell was less than attractive by all accounts of her appearance at 17 when she was set to marry George "Bud" Gollum. However, she was the heiress to a rather sizable estate, and that made her, arguably, a more appealing person. Her father had amassed over $500 000 in wealth through building his family's furniture business and then alter as a real estate developer and financier. This fortune would be worth over $5 million by present day standards.

George, on the other hand, was a handsome, 21-year-old, premed student at Los Angeles City College. He was an ex-Navy man as well, which added to his appeal. He had returned a Pacific War hero and had received the Bronze Star for bravery during the battle of Leyte Gulf.

They seemed like an unlikely couple, but their trail of sordid love letters indicated otherwise.

Whether they were truly in love is anyone's guess. There was evident lust in their relationship. Whether it was simply a case of two young people infatuated with each other to the point of destruction it is hard to determine. The prosecution during their trial certainly tried to prove that was case.

Beulah Louise believed she was in love with George. Despite this, her parents didn't agree with the engagement. They were less than enthusiastic about her fiancé. They claimed to like him well enough, but they were no pleased about how young the couple was and they wanted them both to finish college before pursuing marriage.

Still, the couple announced their engagement to the world and planned on going through with the wedding on April 30th of 1947. And with Beulah Louise's insistence on moving forward with the wedding her parents tried even harder to dissuade her. Perhaps they feared that George only wanted to marry their daughter in such a hurry because of her sizable inheritance, she was the sole heir after all. Or maybe, deep down, they really didn't like him. It is hard to know for sure.

Whatever their reasons, they went as far as threatening to disown Beulah Louise if she went through with the wedding. And still she insisted on moving forward with the wedding as planned. She was madly in love with George and there was nothing that her parents could do to convince her not to marry him. She would go through with it even if it meant losing her family's fortune. He was worth that to her, apparently.

Yacht Ride Gone Wrong

It was around 11pm on March 15, 1947 when things took a turn for the worse for the Overell family. Despite their displeasure over their daughter's choice of fiancé the family had still taken out their 47-foot yacht for some family time.

The was moored in Newport Harbour, California for the evening when Beulah Louise and George took a skiff to shore in pursuit of a midnight snack. They were headed to a late-night burger place on shore. Walter, age 62, and Beulah, age 57, stayed on the yacht while the children went to shore.

When the young couple returned to the pier to retrieve their skiff and head back out to the moored yacht they were greeted by a horrifying sight. The 47-foot yacht, called the Mary E., was smoldering and sinking.

As the young couple were placing orders for burgers the yacht had been blown up by an explosion that "just about blew me out of my bunk," according to F.E. Moore, a retired Los Angeles firefighter whose boat had been moored 75-feet away from the Overells'.

Other searchers soon joined Moore, including Beulah Louise and George, who called out and looked for the bodies of Walter and Beulah as the Mary E. continued to sink into the harbour. It would not be until later, when the coast guard dragged the Mary E. into shallow waters, that the bodies would be located.

Although initial reports called the explosion of the Mary E. and the deaths of Beulah and Walter Overell an accident it did not take long for this narrative to change. After a quick examination of the Mary E. it was determined that the explosion was not caused by gasoline but rather by dynamite.

Had the bomb gone off as intended there would have been no reason or evidence to make anyone suspicious of foul play in the explosion of the yacht. However, a few sticks of dynamite had been left in the engine room, wire to an alarm clock detonator. It was this that gave it all away.

The first explosion, from dynamite in another area of the yacht, was likely supposed to trigger a second explosion that reduced the yacht to nothing but splinters. However, something went wrong after that first explosion and the second one never occurred. Thus, the unexploded dynamite was easily discovered. It was likely the heavy wooden bulkhead of the yacht that caused the second explosive to remain undetonated; still the first explosion was lethal enough.

Walter Overell was found impaled on a plank and Beulah Overell was found with multiple skull fractures. Upon a closer examination by the corner it was discovered that the Overells could have been dead up to an hour before the actual explosion. The cause of death: blunt force trauma. According to the corner a ball-peen hammer fit many of the wound indentations on Beulah Overell's skull.

It was clear that the events of that evening had been no accident. Someone had intentionally murdered the Overells and then planted explosives to cover-up that murder. It didn't take authorities much effort to determine who their prime suspects in this case would be. After all, no one else had been on the yacht that evening with the Overells except for their daughter and future son-in-law. It didn't take a genius to connect those dots.

The Obvious Suspects

It took a day after the explosion for the police to have Beulah Louise and George in custody and charged with murder. It wasn't a large leap to make even with the early evidence.

The parents did not approve of the impending nuptials between the two young lovers. Beulah Louise was set to inherit a large sum of money upon her parents' death. The money alone was motive enough as far as the police were concerned.

In the days following the explosion more evidence came to light that pointed fingers at the young couple. An investigation into Gollum's car revealed wire and pink adhesive tape. The same wire and tape had been found in the set of explosives that had not been detonated on the yacht. Additionally, the police found bloody clothes in his car.

On top of this police found a record of purchase at the Chatsworth office of the Trojan Powder Company that indicated fifty sticks of dynamite had been purchased by the young couple the day before the explosion. The police had been led to the Chatsworth office by a receipt for the purchase that they'd found in Gollum's camera case. On the receipt was a signature of a different name but it was signed by Gollum's hand.

During questioning about the death of her parents Beulah Louise seemed to lack any emotion over their death. Additionally, many people noted the fact that she wore a mink coat when she was taken into custody. And, as with any media heavy case, people took note of Beulah Louise's plump figure, her bush brows, and her inappropriate taste in clothing considering the circumstances.

The case shot to media headlines rather quickly and the young couple were thrust into the spotlight. Everything about their lives were torn apart and exposed to the public eye. Along with all elements pointing towards them, their relationship also raised eyebrows.

They were an unlikely couple. Physically they were poorly matched. In life experience and intelligence they were poorly matched. The only thing that seemed to be pulling them towards each other was an unexplained lust. The police found several love letters penned between the two that pointed to an almost obsessive level of lust.

George wrote to Beulah "I'll kidnap and carry you off somewhere so that no on will ever be able to find us and there I'll make passionate and violent love to you. If you ever marry another person, I will kill him".

Beulah wrote to George "O my darling, O my pops, popsie, darling, my beautiful, handsome, intelligent pops, I adore you always, eternally..."

Their letters expressed an obsessive type of romance that made no sense to those looking in on the relationship. It had likely made no sense to Beulah Louise's parents. It definitely made no sense to the public and it only did more to create intrigue and interest around the trial.

If nothing else, the events of that night caused some interesting gossip for the people of Orange County and dragged some attention away from the aftermath of war and struggle.

The Last Great Trial of Printed Media

The Overell Trial is arguably one of the last spectacular trials of printed media. Before television news took over to inform the citizens of the world what was happening, people had to rely solely on printed press. And the Los Angeles Times carried the story of the trial to the citizens while the more sensationalized version was held within the pages of the Los Angeles Examiner focusing mostly on the young lovers.

Additionally, the New York Times, Life Magazine, dozens of other life interest magazines, and most of the sixty police/detective fact and fiction magazines also covered the case and trial. There was not a piece of printed media that was not scraping to get its hands on any information possible about this case and trial as things proceeded.

There were three main features to every story: the heinousness of the crime, the love between George and Beulah Louise, and the scandal of the rich. It was a journalists dream to be able to write about such a thing.

Parricide was the ultimate breach of the social contract both within the family and without at the time. It was equivocal to regicide in the eyes of many. And although shocking, it was not as rare as many assumed. California had experienced an average of three such cases each year for the past two decades up until that point.

All parricide cases shared some similar traits. The parent or parents, who ultimately ended up being simply the victims, had some form of power over the offenders be it psychological, physical, or financial. It was uncommon for the child to kill their parent(s) with a single wound, thus resulting in multiple and excessive wounds to the victims bodies. These victims are usually shot several times, stabbed several times, or bludgeoned. Sometimes it can be a combination of all three.

There is often such uncontrolled rage present in how these victims are killed that it goes beyond seeking their simple death and seeking their complete destruction. Most individuals who commit parricide want to ensure, beyond any doubt, that their victims are never coming back.

The element of parricide added to the sensationalization of this case in the media. In addition, the hype of the young lovers whose love was not approved of by her parents drew even more attention to it. And finally, top it off with a substantial fortune to be inherited as a result of her parents' death and it was perfect.

Newspapers and magazines practically sold themselves over the four-month trial, the weeks leading up to it, and the time following its conclusion. All of America was focused on what was happening in Orange County and it was a welcomed distraction for many.

The Trial of Overell and Gollum

On March 26, 1947 the Grand Jury returned unanimous indictments of murder against George Gollum and Beulah Louise Overell.

On April 4th, California State Attorney General Fred Howser removed Orange County District Attorney Davis from the prosecution due to his open skepticism over the court case and his past leniency towards women and minors in capital cases. Many members of the prosecution believed that Davis would not be able to fulfill his duties fully considering the elements of the case.

Eugene Williams was named as Special Prosecutor on the case. Williams had recently returned from the Tokyo War Crimes trials where he had successfully prosecuted Premier Tojo and other members of the Japanese wartime government.

Santa Ana Attorney Otto Jacobs, who was formerly the President of the California Bar Association and was well known in local courts, led the defense team. Jacobs was also known to have a reputation as a ruthless and clever litigator who would stop at nothing to get his clients off.

On May 26th the trial began at the Santa Ana Superior Court. Judge Kenneth E. Morrison presided over the trial. It took five weeks to select a jury and 567 prospective jurors were interviewed before a jury of six women and six men was settled upon. The judge had to revive old circuit-court law and sent his bailiffs out to roam the streets of Santa Ana in order to find people to interview for the jury. They had exhausted the voters' rolls and were desperate to get the trial started.

During an unprecedented heat wave, the trial began with the prosecutions opening statements. Williams outlined, quite graphically, the elements of the case. Williams stated, "the defendants enjoyed an illicit, perverted, sadistic sexual passion amounting to...frenzy. Lust, greed, frustration, these are the raw materials of which murders are made".

The burden on the state was to prove that Beulah Louise had beaten her parents to death and then planted explosive on the Mary E. in order to destroy the evidence of the crime. Their focus was on Beulah Louise, as opposed to George, but it was clear that he was associated in some way.

The defense entered two pleas: not guilty and not guilty by reason of insanity. It wasn't as common of a practice as it is not to claim insanity on behalf of female victims, assuming that their actions were driven by fear or rage. At this time the rights of the family took precedent over the rights of the abused child or spouse. Therefore, the insanity plea stood on shaky grounds.

The prosecution needed to prove that the Overells were murdered before the explosion. It was pivotal to their case. Therefore, the prosecution opened their case with forensic evidence. The mortician who had embalmed the bodies originally, stated that he had received the bodies for embalming and believed them to have been dead roughly six hours upon his receipt of them at 2:45am. The mortician claimed that rigormortis had set in, which usually appears within 4-10 hours after death. It was the main way of determining time of death at the time.

The defense criticized the mortician's methodology deeming it inaccurate and unscientific. The defense went on to indicate that the mortician was not a medical professional and therefore did not possess the proper qualifications to make such statements.

Lawrence Mathes, chief residence surgeon of the Orange County Hospital and acting county coroner did have the credentials to make statements about the type of death the Overells endured. He testified for the prosecution stating that the Overells' deaths were the result of multiple skull fractures caused by the explosion and blunt force trauma made by a metal rode, approximately 3-inches in diameter.

The prosecution also brought forward Ray Parker, Los Angeles County Police Department forensic chemist to testify about the explosion. They additionally showed photos of the aftermath of the explosion and the mutilated bodies of the Overells.

These photos were graphic, as Walter's back had been completely torn open in the explosion. One jury member even had to be led out of the courtroom after seeing them. George looked at the photos, but eventually had to turn away from the sight of them. Beulah Louise stared blankly at the photos of her mutilated parents, her face expressionless.

The defense spun their story for the jury. Jacobs asserted that Walter Overell was depressed from his work life and had asked George to get him the dynamite for a suicide attempt. Jacobs went as far as to accuse Dr. Mathes of perjury and brought forward his own experts to indicate that the explosion and nothing more caused the deaths of the Overells.

It was a risky move, but it was enough to throw a shadow of doubt on the prosecutions forensic evidence. And that was all that they really needed to do. The prosecutions case hinged on their forensic evidence and if it couldn't hold up then they simply had no case.

On August 25th Beulah Louise took the witness stand and testified that she had no involvement in the death of her parents. On August 27th George took the stand and said the same.

On October 5th, after 19 weeks and 107 witnesses the jury announced a verdict of not guilty.

The Sensational Verdict

A verdict of not guilty made headlines across the country. The young couple would walk free. They were potential murders, but the court system had spoke. The trial was done and that was the end of it.

The verdict was surprising, but realistically not at all. The jury was pulled from the Orange County middle and working class citizens. The prosecution and the Overells were outsiders to them. The case was riddled with lies and controversy. The evidence was unclear and there was no way to know beyond a reasonable doubt that Beulah Louise and George had done it.

The only thing that the jury was certain of was that the couple was entitled to their legal innocence until proven guilty. And as far as the jury was concerned the prosecution had failed to do just that.

The trial was riddled with spectacles during its four-month run. There were issues with jury-tampering, treats of death, and assault to jurors. There were also citizens showing up scantily clad to get their fifteen minutes of fame. The longer the trial went on the more strange things happened. It was a different time and it was the biggest case that had been seen in a long time.

Newport Police Captain Harry Lace was the office in charge of the case. When interviewed about the case later in life (1989) he stated "the past is a foreign country: they do things differently there..."

Captain Harry Lace left the police force in 1958 and was never associated with the brutality, corruption, and harassment that became associated with the force in the 1960s. He always believed that Beulah

Louise and George were guilty, and believed he could prove it. But the prosecution had mishandled the case, especially the physical evidence. And from a legal standpoint they "deserved to go free" according to Harry.

That was the only thing anyone could agree on in relation to the trial. Did they do it? No one could really say for certain. It would never be proven. And the case would be closed from that point on. There would be no justice for Walter and Beulah Overell. There would be no finite conclusion to their murders. It will always be one of those cases that will be examined, speculated about, and ultimately remain a mystery.

The Aftermath for Beulah Louise Overell

After the trial ended in a verdict of not guilty, despite the heavy media attention, there was nothing else to do. The prosecution had lost the case and they did not have the means to file an appeal. No one else was arrested for the deaths of Walter and Beulah Overell; no one was even investigated. As far as the police department was concerned the case was closed and would remain that way.

Beulah Louise went on to inherit her parents' estate, which was valued over $500 000 at the time. Not too bad for some one who was still in her teens. She and Bud never did get married. After the four-month long trial things between the couple had cooled off and the two of them went their separate ways. This was likely the most shocking to the public considering how sordid and passionate their romance had seemed. A murder trial can put quite a damper on an engagement it would seem, no matter how much money is involved.

Beulah Louise married twice after the trial, but she was dead by 1965 at the young age of 36. The cause of her death was apparent acute alcoholism according to the news reports on the case. Her nude, bruised body was found in her bed of her Las Vegas home with two empty bottles of vodka. She also, apparently, had a loaded, cocked, but unfired .22-calibre rifle at her feet. She left no children to inherit whatever was left of her parents' estate.

The Aftermath for George Gollum

An interview done in 1988 found George Gollum to be the divorced father of two children (a girl and a boy). He completed a Ph.D. in biophysics under an assumed name after abandoning his career in medicine due to the press coverage from the trial. It didn't matter that he hadn't been convicted; respectable people did not act like that and did not get accused of such things.

He had spent some time with a carnival after the trial and ended up spending nine months in the federal prison in Tallahassee, although there are no prison records to confirm this. He even married a carnival girl right after the trial, but that marriage was annulled. He was later married for 20 years to the mother of his children.

Now George, having abandoned the nickname "Bud", enjoys flying small airplanes, photography, and fishing. He lives in a small town outside of Sierra, Nevada. He was 62-years-old at the time of the interview and heavily involved in the real estate business in western America after having an earlier career making over-the-shoulder weapons with the Navy.

He is content to answer questions about what happened in his life all those years ago, but does not provide more than the briefest of responses. And as for those who still believe that he played a role in the death of his future in-laws? George firmly believes, as he did at the time of the trial, that those who knew him knew that he was not capable of such a thing and the others he has no control over. Otherwise, he continues to live his life, raise his children, and try to leave the past in the past.

KIM SNIBSON

"Why is this happening?"

Those may have been Greg Hosa's last audible words as Andrew Flentjar and Stacy Lea-Caton brutally forced him to the ground. The answer Flentjar gave would shock not just Hosa, but both of his attackers. For it was that response that would have allowed both Flentjar and Lea-Caton to realize that they were not part of the just cause they had believed themselves to be, but were in fact at the mercy of Kim Snibson's deluded and volatile plan.

Kim Snibson is a master manipulator who was envious of the life Greg Hosa and his wife Kathryn McKay had built together. Most notably, their horse farm. Situated in Nowra, New South Wales, Champagne Shires would be considered a small property when compared to the amount of land horse farms usually covered. Still, despite its modest size, it was far grander that Snibson could ever hope to own herself. For her, Champagne Shires was the perfect combination of all her fondest desires and life passions. Living next door to her dream made reality, it didn't take long for her fantasies of owning the property to become a perceived right. Snibson's greed led her to believe that she deserved Champagne Shires, while her ego convinced her that she could have it, if only the current owners were dealt away with.

Once Hosa and McKay had agreed to stable her horse, Snibson had the perfect excuse to visit her neighbors. She would come by often and grew to know both Hosa and McKay well. This access only fuelled her lust for the property and her disdain for the happy owners. Unaware of Snibson's feelings towards them, Hosa and McKay remained kind and generous to their neighbor. On one known occasion, Snibson had fallen behind in payments and owed the couple $300 for the care of her horse. Hosa and McKay had agreed to continue to stable her horse and told Snibson that she could pay them when she was able. This generosity did not provoke gratitude in Snibson, but instead fed into her increasing resentment. By this time she had begun to believe that she could force the couple to sign over the rights to Champagne Shires to her, kill them, and live happily on the property without consequence. Rationally this plan is ludicrous, but given her past success, Snibson believed it to be perfect.

Years earlier Snibson had inherited her house in Calymea Street, Nowra Hill, from an elderly woman named Judith Plankas. It was this property that had made her a neighbor of Hosa and McKay, and ultimately, it was in this house that the couple would be murdered. But it wasn't until after her arrest that questions began to arise as to exactly why and how Ms Plankas came to deed the property to Snibson.

In an interview with Take-5 Magazine, Snibson's ex-husband recalled how Ms Snibson had befriended Ms Plankas. At the time, the elderly dog breeder had been diagnosed with cancer and had needed help taking care of her animals. Snibson had been quick to offer assistance and for a while must have struck the sickly Ms Plankas as a Godsend. But, as Mr Snibson told Take-5 Magazine, "Kim got hold of powerful tranquilizers and quietly killed the older dogs." Perhaps accustomed to Kim's crueler actions, or blinded by devotion, it is believed that Mr Snibson neglected to inform Plankas of what Kim had done. By all appearances, Ms Plankas had no idea what kind of woman she had welcomed into her home.

"Then on April 17, 2003," Mr Snibson recalled, "Judith's condition suddenly worsened. She changed her will that night, leaving the house to Kim, and died the next day."

This would not be the first time Mr Snibson had been privy to the threat Kim posed to those around her. And it would not be the only time his failure to believe or act lead to disastrous consequences. In the same interview, he revealed a conversation he had once had with a woman named Rebecca. She had only been 15-years-old when Ms Snibson had convinced her to move out of the home and in with the Snibson family.

"We've got a free babysitter," Ms Snibson had announced when she had brought the teenager home, according to her ex-husband. He went on to say that, "later, Rebecca sought me out and what she had to say rocked me. Kim had kept a horse at a stable owned by an elderly couple and Rebecca said (that Kim) talked about tying them up, making them sign over their property to her and killing them."

Still, it would seem that Mr Snibson was not then willing to believe his wife capable of such things. But Rebecca wasn't

Snibson's first nor only attempt at recruiting accomplices in her murder plot. Nor was the teenager's confession the only one to be dismissed. Armed with vicious lies and a willingness to manipulate all those around her, Snibson approached numerous people. Perhaps it is a testament to her skill at manipulation, or her ability to choose those reluctant to cause a stir without any solid evidence, but many of the people she approached never spoke of the conversations until after she had been arrested. Mr Snibson claimed that was when he began to receive calls from dozens of friends, most of which started with 'I've been wanting to tell you this for years'.

"Then they'd tell me about an affair she'd had or how she'd tried to enlist them in a desperate scheme to have someone beaten up or killed," he told Take-5 Magazine. He also spoke about how a friend had told him that 'Kim had wanted an old lady beaten up because she said her son had molested one of your girls'. "Nobody has touched my daughters," Mr Snibson said. "It was a fantasy made up by Kim to get others to do terrible things for her."

With so many people aware of the true, malicious nature of Snibson, it is baffling how few people voiced their concerns to law enforcement. Snibson continued her search for willing participants until she found two men who believed her lies. Her first recruit was Andrew Flentjar. He was a neighbor of the Snibson family, although Mr Snibson insists that he didn't know Flentjar that well, and had believed that Snibson hadn't either.

"She didn't socialize with (him) or stay for a cuppa," he had said in an interview. But still Snibson had managed to make the otherwise reasonable man willing to help her in her plan to kidnap and assault Mr Hosa.

"Andrew was told by Kim that the couple had sexually abused her child and had videoed the episode," Paul Leask, a Crown Prosecutor for New South Wales, reviled on the television show Deadly Women.

In her interview on the same television show, a journalist for Illawarra Mercury Newspaper, Veronica Apap, attested that there had been "no evidence at any time in court that Kathryn or Greg had engaged in anything like that." Still, Flintjar believed the story Snibson wove and, under the impression that her plan only involved minor assault as justice for her daughter, agreed to help.

Snibson then approached Stacy Lea-Caton, a former neighbor who had been in trouble with the law. Mr Snibson remembers Lea-Caton as being a man who continuously worked to create a notable reputation for himself as a dangerous man.

"You would be talking about normal things," Mr Snibson told Ms Apap during an interview, "and Stacey would come in with something bigger or better. He talked about his criminal history, stuff like that."

Mr Snibson went on to say that when it came to Mr Lea-Caton he "didn't believe anything he told me", and that, "I didn't think he would go very well in a fight, myself. He is not this tough person he was making himself out to be."

Ms Snibson, however, saw a potential for violence in Lea-Caton and knew just how to bring it to the surface. During a visit she tested the waters by telling him a lie similar to the one she had recruited Flintjar with. According to Leask, "Stacey Lea-Caton was told by her that the couple had drugged her, sexually assaulted her, and videoed the episode."

Once again there she could produce any evidence in support of her claims, nor could later investigators. According to Apap, "It seems to be a total fantasy on her part" and Mr Snibson has stated that "Greg Hosa was a thoroughly decent person who did not deserve such terrible lies to be made up about him, let alone die so needlessly." Still, Snibson was convincing enough to for Lea-Coton to push aside his desire to get his life back on track and he soon found himself alongside Flintjar, embroiled in Snibson's supposed plan for vigilante justice.

"She employed a means of modulating the story depending on the person who was the recipient of it. To press the right buttons." Leask asserted. "The theme was always one of sexual impropriety and of course, nothing excites people's sympathy more than that."

With her two accomplices waiting for instructions, Snibson put her plan into action on January 28th, 2006. It was easy to lure Hosa to her home. The 56-year-old man didn't suspect that anything might be wrong when Snibson called and asked him to come over.

"He came quickly after that conversation occurred," Apap said in her Deadly Women interview. "He didn't think that he was in any danger or that there would be any problem."

Lea-Carton and Flintjar swarmed Hosa as he entered the Snibson home. Using a slab of wood they struck him on the head and forced him to the ground. The men then proceeded to hogtie Hosa, forcing him onto his stomach and binding his legs to his hands. It was during this attack that Hosa asked his assailants "why is this happening?" While the exact wording cannot be determined, it is reported that Flintjar responded by accusing Hosa of pedophilia.

With this declaration both of Snibson's henchmen realized that they had been lied to. They were blindsided by the revelation yet, having participated in assault and kidnapping, and still unaware of just how malicious Snibson's intentions were, neither felt they were in a position to leave. Snibson deceit had taken them past the point of no return and both were at a loss at what to do next. This afforded Snibson the perfect environment to maintain control.

While the men watched over a struggling Hosa, Snibson called his wife and 'confessed' that she and Hosa had been having an affair. It was a story that few would believe and later would be seen by their family as adding a foul insult to considerable injury. Jan Keily, a sister of McKay, would attest that they family was 'disgusted' by the claim. But on that night, it was enough to draw McKay into Snibon's trap.

Just like her husband, 44-year-old McKay was set upon by Lea-Carton and Flintjar. She too was hogtied and gagged by having a sock forced into her mouth and taped into place. Once again the men found themselves forced into a situation far from what they had been expecting when Snibson left to retrieve two 44-gallon drums from Champagne Shires and brought them to the house.

After shoving Ms McKay into one of the drums Snibson disclosed the needlessly cruel method she had chosen in order to kill McKay. "She murdered Kathryn by wrapping tape around her face and eyes and nose," Leask described.

Many factors must be considered when determining how long it would take an individual to suffocate to death. First, oxygen deprivation renders the victim unconscious. If they are still unable to breath brain damage will begin. As a general guide, it is believed to take approximately 5-6 minutes for death to occur. Snibson, Lea-Carton, and Flintjar stood by and watched McKay struggle for this entire length of time. When arrested, all three would give varying statements as to what exactly had happened that night, but in all versions, the two men who had not agreed to murder still made no attempt to save Ms McKay.

When Snibson turned her attention back to Hosa, she had a different method in mind for his execution. According to Leask, "Kim killed Greg Hosa by garrotting him with electrical wire. Kim killed them both deliberately and methodically." And once again, her now reluctant accomplices failed to put an end to her actions.

As night fell the trio loaded the two barrels, each now filled with the corpses of a once loving couple, into the back of Snibson's truck. Together the three drove to a remote patch of the Tomerong State Forest. Here she doused the remains of Ms McKay and Mr Hosa with petrol and set them alight.

As Leask stated, "Incinerating the bodies was done for no other purpose than to destroy evidence that those two poor people had ever been to Kim's house that day."

For all her obsession and manipulation, it took only hours for Snibson's plan to come undone. As it would turn out, Mr Snibson's reading of Stacey Lea-Caton's character had been far more reliable that Kim's had been. The only known criminal within the trio, Lea-Carton was unable to suppress his guilty conscious and within hours of leaving Snibson confessed to his sister and her husband. The series of events he told them had been highly edited but it was still damning enough that the young couple had insisted that he tell the authorities. At 2:30am they had taken him to the Nowra Police Station to report the crime. According to police, Lea-Caton had originally stated that he had seen a man and woman tried up at the farm and was worried that they might come to harm. By 8:00am they had arrested Snibson. A whole day hadn't passed by the time police located the remains of Greg Hosa and Kathryn McKay. Superintendent Kyle Stewart would describe the discovery as a "horrific scene", while Leask provided greater detail. "All that remained of Kathryn was her right foot and little remained of Greg."

But even when caught Snibson was far from willing to admit to her actions. In her statements to the police, she was a hapless witness to a domestic disturbance that spiraled out of control. According to Snibson, she had informed Ms McKay that she had been having an affair with Mr Hosa. Hosa had come to her home first, followed by and enraged Ms McKay. Once there, the couple had begun to argue. The confrontation soon grew volatile and in the heat of the moment Lea-Caton had picked up a bird perch and struck Mr Hose over the head hard enough that he fell to the ground. She recounted how this hadn't deterred Ms McKay who had then turned her anger onto Snibson herself. McKay had become so furious that she had 'come at' Snibson. This had forced Flentjar, who had also happened to be present, to tackle the older woman to keep her from harming Snibson.

"She fell back and hit her head on the pantry and fell on the floor," Snibson told police. She further went on to explain that is was after Ms McKay had been injured that Lea-Caton's murderous intent rose to the surface. In Snibson's version of events, it was Lea-Caton that strangled Hosa with a rope before forcing her to wrap tape around McKay's head until, as she insisted he had instructed, 'she turned blue'. In his final act of depravity, Lea-Caton had been the one to light the bodies on fire.

Her behavior at the trials of her accomplices was a far cry from what others had observed during her own trial. While giving evidence in the New South Wales Supreme Court, Snibson broke down into tears as she described the "gurgling sounds" Mr Hosa made as the life was choked out of him. Snibson would tell the court that she felt "sick to my stomach" about the murders. She continued to say that she thought about it "every single day." She had become so unsettled that Justice Terence Buddin had to adjourn the sentencing hearing for five minutes to give her time to compose herself.

Compared to her behavior and demeanor at other times it was almost possible to believe Ms Snibson was two entirely different people. For Leask, there was no doubt which persona was ligament and which she put on for self-preservation.

"There will be no remorse from Kim Snibson. It's not in her nature," he had said in an interview. He also claimed that Snibson is a person "that lacks the quality that makes us human beings." But perhaps his opinion on Snibson was most elegantly and directly described within his statement, "I have been involved in some shocking crimes involving some dreadful brutality. This case stands out because, in my career, I can only reasonably expect to come across one or two sociopaths. And that's what Kim Snibson is."

It is a sentiment echoed by Candice DeLong, a former criminal profiler for the Federal Bureau of Investigation who often lends her insights to programs such as Deadly Women. "It's unlikely Kim feels remorse for what she did. Sociopaths never do," she said during an interview. She further asserted that "if she ever does emerge from prison, watch out."

It is DeLong's opinion that "Kim is a natural born killer. She wanted to commit murder," but for those like her ex-husband, Snibson is not so clearly an evil woman. While he called her 'pure evil' in an interview with Take-5 Magazine it was also discovered that he had withheld information from investigators in a bid to protect her from prosecution.

"I did tell the truth in all statements," he told the New South Wales Supreme Court. "I left out those couple of sentences from Kim because it sounded very damning to me. I didn't want to see anything bad happen to her. I still had loyalty to Kim even though we had long broken up."

Some of these omitted sentences referred to statements Ms Snibson had made the day after her arrest. According to Mr Snibson, she had said "Don't worry about me, I'm a bad person", and had alluded that she would be 'going away' for 30 years. He further stated that Snibson had said that while she did want to tell him what had happened on the night of the murders her lawyer had instructed her not to talk about it. "She said when she gets to court and has her say, the truth will come out."

Whether Mr Snibson truly believes in his ex-wife's innocence or not, he unwittingly brought more evidence against her. When Detective Sergeant Jason Hogan had asked Mr Snibson to take them to where he as Ms Snibson used to train their dogs for dog sled competitions he had agreed. The location he had led them to had been the where the smoldering barrels holding the remains of McKay and Hosa had been found. In the same day, he had also unknowingly brought the police to the part of Braidwood Road where Mr Hosa's burnt out four-wheel drive had been discovered.

Andrew Wayne Flentjar was the first to be sentenced. He is currently serving a minimum of 10-years for his role in assisting in the kidnapping of Hosa and McKay. Stacey Lea-Caton pleaded guilty to aiding and abetting murder and received a sentence of a minimum 16 years, with the maximum time served of 22-years.

Lea-Caton testified against Snibson during her trail and put a great amount of pressure on her supposed version of events. Combined with the sight of the 44-gallon drums, similar to those used to dispose of McKay and Hosa's remains, which were brought into the courtroom, the cracks in Snibson's account of that night were beginning to show. Whatever the 10 men and 2 women of the jury had truly believed was rendered moot when, approximately halfway through her trial, Snibson changed her plea to guilty.

On September 5th, 2008 Snibson faced her sentencing hearing. By Australian law, those affected by a crime have the right to lodge and read out a victim impact statement to the court and the perpetrator. The friends and family of Hosa and McKay took advantage of this opportunity. Marion, Katheryn McKay's sister, described how the murders had rendered her family into a state similar to 'animals caught in headlights'. In her statement, she explained how she struggled "to find the words for the numbness and traumatic feelings the murders caused the family."

Marion described the impact of their loss and Snibson's actions as being felt "physically, socially, emotionally and psychologically." How her family is no longer able to watch programs about horses or the news, as they stir up too many painful memories. How her work as a counselor has suffered and that the majority of her grief-stricken family has since abandoned their homes in Nowra.

She described McKay and Hosa as loving, community-minded people, and reminded the court and Snibson that her sister had been a nurse with a natural drive and desire to help other people. She reiterated how their senseless and brutal deaths have had a lasting impact on hundreds of other people and how more than 500 people had attended their funerals. Somewhere within this speech, Kim Snibson reportedly began to cry.

Another of McKay's sisters, Jan Keily, spoke of her utter confusion at how Snibson, Flintjar, and Lea-Caton could have brought themselves to do what they had done. She also addressed how insulting it was to the memories or their loved ones that Snibson still maintained that there had been an affair, not to mention the accusations she had made about McKay's intended violence towards Snibson. "The families are shocked by the lies that have been told about Kathryn McKay and Gregory Hosa by the three offenders."

Justice Buddin commended the sisters for the dignity and grace they had shown while delivering their statements before adjourning the proceedings. When he delivered the final verdict, Justice Buddin gave his own opinion on the case before him. He expressed how the crimes against this kind-hearted couple had been committed with a "considerable degree of callousness".

Justice Buddin explored the suffering that was inflicted upon Mr Hosa and Ms McKay, not just at the agonizingly slow and painful death, but at the mental torture that must have endured at the hands of the captors. He expressed how they were forced to wait for a "not inconsiderable amount of time", stuck in a state of anguish, wondering what their kidnappers would decide to do to them. "They were totally defenseless and at the mercy of the offenders," he said.

Justice Buddin then turned his attention to the version of events that Snibson had put forth, the version of events that left her as a victim of circumstances and Lea-Coton's vicious nature. He described this story as "implausible", "quite fanciful" and "tailored to suit inescapable, objective facts". As proof of the ridiculousness of her claims, he pointed to her recruitment of accomplices. This was not an act of a woman caught off guard by a lover's spat but instead was indicative of the level of calculation and manipulation she was capable of wilfully wielding.

While Snibson had told the court that she was sorry for the role she had played in the couple's grizzly end, Justice Buddin was not swayed. He explained that he had not believed her words to be those of someone truly remorseful and repentant, but instead said that whatever contrition she had expressed struck him as contrived. His final verdict had been a jail sentence of no less than 32 years. This means that

Snibson would be 60-years-old before she becomes eligible to apply for parole.

The town of Nowra is still healing from the horrors of that singular night. As Paul Leask has stated, "that one of their own was the killer was something that psychologically traumatized that community." The senseless cruelty Snibson brought down upon a devoted, generous couple has only been magnified by the ridiculousness of her plan. For all the action she was willing to take there was no way her plan would allow her to gain ownership of Champagne Shire, rendering her depraved actions useless and her goal unattainable.

But perhaps what is hardest for the residents of Nowra, and all that hear of the tragic deaths of McKay and Hosa, to come to terms with, is the wealth of opportunities presented for people to intervene. Be it out of embarrassment or social delicacy, those who had concerns over Sibson's actions had refused to disclose what they had known. At the time it might have been dismissed as a personal eccentricity, a misunderstanding, or a benign threat, but now blaze as warning signs for the brutality that was to come. Perhaps if those who had felt the inkling of concern had stepped forward a different course could have been plotted and McKay and Hosa could have been spared. But then it is also possible that nothing could have deterred Snibson, and that these murders were the only end her insatiable greed would have allowed. Wherever the truth may lie, it is too late to act for McKay and Hosa. Their lives have already been sacrificed on the altar of Snibson's pride. The only solace that is to be garnished now is that Snibson has been removed from the general population and will hopefully be unable to claim any further victims. But what little comfort this offers will forever be overshadowed by the influence Snibon's name will forever provoke. Those who learn about the merciless crimes this woman visited upon the people who would have been her friends will undoubtedly no longer be able to look at their neighbors without there being the lingering question of 'what if?'

HUSBAND KILLER SHEENA EASTBURN

86

JAIMI WEST

Sheena Eastburn seemed to have the cards stacked against her from the start. She and Tim Eastburn were married young, when she had only just turned fifteen. The couple wed in 1990, although Tim was older, at twenty-one years of age. Talking many years later to the Joplin Globe, Alica Blevins- Sheena's mother- talked about how she should have guided her daughter's life differently, and put her on a different path.

"She was only 15 then. She was just a kid... Sheena was wild. I will admit that," she said. "For her and Tim, life was one big party. "She got herself in situations that got her into a lot of trouble. There were a lot of things that happened to her as a child that she never told me.

I just wish I could have done more for her when I had the chance. Maybe things would have turned out differently."

They were divorced a short two years later, which is often the case for couples married at such a young age.

While the divorce was described by friends as amicable, the couple maintained a sexual relationship over the years. Both were heavy drinkers, and took drugs together. In fact, whenever Sheena needed a fix, friends said, she would visit her ex-husband and provide sexual favours in return for drugs. The couple were still so close that they discussed remarriage.

Speaking about their relationship, Sheena would later say: "There were days when he loved me more than you could ever imagine and there were other days when we just fought. I was 15 years old when we got married. He was like a father and a husband to me. He was a wonderful man."

On or around November 1st, 1991, Sheena met Terry Banks for the first time, and the two immediately became close. When Banks learned of Sheena's continuing relationship with her ex-husband, however, he became "extremely possessive, jealous, and violent" according to court records. This was the catalyst for Tim's murder.

Tim Eastburn's murder

Tim was murdered using his own rifle, on November 19th 1992. He was shot in his own home in McDonald County, Missouri. The house is set a little back from the road, among the wooded hills common in McDonald County.

At the time of the murder, Sheena had only just turned seventeen, and her co-defendants were nineteen (Banks) and eighteen as well (Myers).

Two days previously, Sheena's co-defendants, Terry Banks and Matt Myers, had stolen Tim's gun- an AK-47- in a break-in along with a third man named Denashay, or 'D.J'. Johnson. They also took the chance to steal some of Tim's valuables, since stealing the gun on its own would have appeared suspicious.

The burglary took place only two weeks after Sheena had begun secretly dating her fellow co-defendant, Terry Banks. Tim and Sheena, Banks, Myers and Johnson were in fact all part of the same large circle of friends. In the time building up to the murder, the group had been drinking to excess and using drugs, a fact which probably gave the defendants the courage to do what they were about to do.

On the evening of November 19th, Sheena, Banks and Myers paid a visit to Tim at his home. It was only on that day that Sheena learned of the burglary at all; Myers and Banks had said they wanted to sell the gun- which would have fetched a good price- but Sheena convinced them not to, since it could be traced back to Tim through the serial number.

Sheena went in at first, alone, to talk with him. She asked him if he would like to come outside to take a ride on her motorbike, but he refused, saying that it was too late at night for him to want to go out.

At the time, Banks and Myers were hiding on the front porch. As Tim and Sheena continued talking, they walked through the house to the kitchen, where the pair kissed. It was only seconds later that Tim was shot with his own gun, through the window, by one of the pair outside. He quickly fell to the floor, and as he lay, Myers ran into the house to shoot him again to 'finish him off'. As he shot Tim for the second and final time, Sheena and Terry Banks ran from the house.

According to later interviews with Sheena, Tim's last words were "God forgive me for all my sins."

All three were arrested only days later, and each confessed separately to their role in Tim's murder. Each of their confessions were coherent, and none of the defendants contradicted the others with regards to their description of the day's events. However, Banks and Myers both claimed that Sheena had come up with the plot to murder Tim, a claim that she denied.

The Trial

Sheena was in prison for three years by the time she was finally put up for trial.

The facts of Tim Eastburn's murder were not challenged in court by either Terry Banks or Matt Myers. The only challenge made by Sheena was whether her actions were made after 'deliberation and cool reflection' or not- which is the metric by which murder in the first degree is judged under Missouri law. However, the defence also argued that Sheena did not necessarily understand her co-defendants' murderous intentions beforehand, a fact which also would have lessened the charge against her.

In testimony for her defence, Sheena claimed that she only learned of the burglary on the day of the murder itself. She believed that on the day that Tim died, the group of three were going to steal money and drugs from her ex-husband. She denied any knowledge of a plot to kill him. "I was supposed to go down there and get him out of the house, then we were going rob him for drugs and money."

They also planned to leave the gun at Tim's house after the robbery, rather than arouse suspicion by selling it. Sheena was quoted in interviews long after the trial, still standing by what she said. "The intent was to take back the gun that was stolen. They could track it down.

The timeline of the day's events suggested otherwise, however. Sheena's request for her ex-husband to follow her outside, and her bringing him to the kitchen with a window to the front of the house, suggested that she was trying to lead him to her death. At the very least, it was clear that it wasn't Sheena who fired the fatal shots from Tim's own gun. She claimed that Banks had shot him first in a fit of passion, after seeing the pair kiss. Myers had then delivered the final bullet.

After the shot was fired, Sheena said, "[w]e both dropped and when we dropped I crawled around to where he was, and I tried to stop the bleeding. There was nothing I could do." She was trying to paint a picture of innocence. She later talked about how she had tried to stop the bleeding with a towel and a sock that were lying nearby.

Over the course of the trial, extensive physical evidence was used in attempt to prove the group's guilt, almost sixty items in total. These included the rifle and the fragments of bullets found in Tim's body-which matched- and photo after photo of the crime scene.

D.J. Johnson also testified to the effect that the murder had been pre-meditated. He was actually a witness for the prosecution throughout the trial, as part of a plea bargain to help secure the verdicts of murder against the other three. As a result of his actions, he was given probation in connection to the charges of burglary against him, as he was part of the group that stole Tim's AK-47.

He testified that on the day of the murder itself, he overheard a three-way conversation between Myers, Banks and Sheena. In that conversation, Sheena discussed Tim with the others, claiming that he had raped her, and that she would love to see him dead. Banks, her then boyfriend, and Myers then both volunteered their services, according to Johnson. Sheena's attorneys made no attempt to discredit him, or disagree with any of his testimony.

The defence, however, argued that his testimony was unreliable due to its acquisition through a plea bargain. Johnson was offered freedom in exchange for his witness statements, and this perhaps did cast doubt on the truth of what he said. However, it was left for the jury to decide just what to make of his claims, and his statements formed a key part of the prosecution's case.

Prison Time

Whether the jury's decision would have been changed by any of this information must forever remain unknown. What they did decide, after a gruelling six hours, was that Sheena was guilty of first-degree murder.

Matt Myers was sentenced as the man who, according to the three confessions, had fired both of the fatal shots. Although he was only charged with second degree murder, among other offences related to Tim's murder (i.e. the burglary), he was sent to prison for a total of 67 years. Because of the murder being judged as of the second degree, he was eligible for parole throughout his sentence.

Terry Banks on the other hand, was sent to prison for life, on a charge of first degree murder. Sheena, too, was jailed with the same charge. The fact that Banks and Sheena were charged with first degree murder, whereas Myers (who fired one of the shots that killed Tim) wasn't, seems strange in hindsight. But Myers had made a plea bargain that saw him receive 'only' 67 years, but with the chance for parole in the future.

Indeed, Sheena's attorney filed a motion for post conviction relief in the immediate aftermath of the sentence, but this motion was denied.

"I really believed I was going to get second degree murder and I was accountable for that. I was okay with that," Sheena said in an interview, years later. She was visibly stunned when she learned of her sentence. "All I could hear was my mother in the courtroom... She was wailing," Sheena told KOAM TV. As part of the same news segment, Sheena's mother Alica Bleavins remembered the same scene: "I couldn't control it. When that's your child, and your only child, and your hands are tied..."

Terry Banks' story became more interesting in the year 2000, when he escaped from his maximum-security prison with the help of a guard. Lynnette Barnett smuggled Banks out in broad daylight, with the help of an old uniform and a fake ID. They were on the run for six weeks before they were caught. She was jailed for five years, with the help of video evidence and correspondence between her and Banks. She was, however, paroled within a year of her sentence.

Banks had another 16 years added to his sentence, although since he was already in prison for life with no option of parole, it makes little difference.

At the time of the escape, Sheena's mother said: "They put her on lock-down. They put her in the hole. They were going to leave her there until he was captured. The FBI, well, they were all over Sheena. She was the one who told them his dad was in Texas."

Signs of hope for Sheena?

There were several facts and allegations which weren't raised at trial, that in hindsight, should have been. Sheena's attorneys spoke publicly about how the outcome may have been completely different had they brought them up.

For one, IQ tests performed by Sheena in the buildup to the trial suggested that she would be incapable of organising the events as described by the prosecution.

There were also allegations that she had been raped by a McDonald County Jail when awaiting trial, and even taken to an abortion clinic. A guard who had been working there, Terrie Zornes, had been accused by Sheena of manipulating and raping her several times over the course of her time there. He had been 31, whereas she was still a minor.

Sheena claimed that he had taken her twice to the property room in 1994, and attacked her there. He was the only guard on duty at the time. According to interviews, Sheena had told her mother: "I told my mother that the officer had taken me to a property closet and had sex with me. She flipped out at that point. They locked me down in my cell.

Cut off my phone. I wasn't allowed to talk to anybody. They cut off my visitors."

Multiple reviews of the surveillance tape from the nights that Sheena alleged she had been raped gave suspicious results. While nothing of note happened, at one point in the recordings the clock would jump forward. "The hands on the clock jumped forward. A clock doesn't do that," The Sheriff of McDonald County Jail later said.

The Sherriff had nonetheless defended Zornes, claiming that the sex was "consensual". Altogether, it seemed as if both the guard and the Sheriff felt that there was something to hide.

Sheena responded with revealing comments about her past. "They kept trying to tell me it was consensual. They said: 'You know you wanted it. You know you miss it.' It was not like I fought it because there was no way I could have stopped him. I have experienced sexual abuse all of my life. I have been raped before in a violent way. After you have been in that situation, you just learn it's easier to let it go and not fight."

Moreover, in the years since the case was closed, Myers recanted on his testimony at the trial that Sheena had been the mastermind of the operation. Kent Gipson, Sheena's long time attorney, had even attained an affidavit to that effect- and that he had acquired the same from Johnson, too. This would mean that in conjunction with their defence stemming from the low IQ test score, it would be possible to argue that Sheena could not have possibly wanted Tim to be killed that day.

These facts all gave Sheena hope that she could appeal her sentence, and perhaps, win. Even if she were only able to replace her sentence with one for second degree murder, she would at least be eligible for parole in the end.

Supreme Court challenge

In interviews after her sentencing, Sheena said: "I still thought that I might get out of prison someday... I didn't realize that life without parole actually meant life without parole." She continued to maintain her innocence, saying that she had never planned a murder that day, only a robbery.

In 2012, a case went through the Alabama Supreme Court which found that the sentence of life without parole was actually unconstitutional when handed down to a minor. The case came from Alabama, but because it had been decided by the Supreme Court, cases could now be challenged nationwide. Missouri, at the time, had 84 cases of juveniles jailed for life without parole and each one of them could now seek to have their sentences reduced.

Suddenly, it seemed that Sheena might have found a way out. Once more, Sheena contacted her attorney, and they began to prepare her case for appeal. Talking to KOAM TV, her attorney Kent Gipson said "I think if you look across the spectrum of persons convicted of first degree murder, I'd say her level of culpability is among the lowest I've ever seen."

Sheena's attorney believed that she had a great chance to finally be considered for parole; and both clearly believed that she deserved the chance. "I think inevitably she will be given a parolable sentence and will be given a chance to get out of prison," Gipson said at the time. Speaking about the progress she had made while in prison, he said "She's obviously not the same person she was when she was 17 years old, I don't think any of us are... She is probably the most ideal candidate for parole any of them [prison staff] have ever seen.""

Miles Parks, a retired investigator who had worked on the case, disagreed. "Sheena Eastburn was old enough to get a driver's license, old enough to get married, old enough to know the difference between right and wrong," Parks said. "What do you think is the appropriate punishment?"

In an interview before her appeal with KOAM TV, she talked about the possibility that she might be released. "I came to that realization a long time ago, and I gave it to God, and I got peace," she had said. She still maintained that she had no role in Tim's murder, saying that "[t]here was no reason for Tim to die... None."

With her interviewer, she discussed what she missed about the outside world: "...going down to the refrigerator in the middle of the night and being able to get what you want. Walking barefoot on grass somewhere that it doesn't say 'out of bounds'. Going outside after dark. Just taking time to experience free, fresh air... I know it smells different on the other side."

Sheena wished that she could somehow find release. But she still refused to get her hopes up, stating that "You never count on anything completely until it happens because you can't let yourself get your hopes too high and then be devastated all the time. It's just a hard way to live." Over her time in prison, she had clearly lived with a hope that one day she would be set free, but had only been disappointed.

The Post-Conviction Hearing

Close friends and relatives of Tim's did not want the case re-opened. Speaking in an interview, Bobby Eastburn said, "We have been keeping track of it. We don't like what is going on. She worked hard to get in there and we don't want her out of prison. "My brother won't get a second chance. She's apparently trying to get a second chance. They say she was suffering from PTSD because of her childhood and that she was not very smart. She manipulated the situation to kill Tim. She was the mastermind behind it. She was intelligent enough to set the whole situation up."

On April 30th of 2013, three cases of minors jailed for life were put before the Missouri Supreme Court- one of them being Sheena's. Her attorney argued that the original motion that had been filed way back in 1992, for post conviction relief, should not have been denied. They argued that the judge should have then realised that such a sentence was unconstitutional.

The state argued that they did not then have the authority to challenge the constitutionality of the sentence, and so they were correct to not have allowed the defendant's motion for relief. After both sides had been presented, the court took recess so that the judges could decide on their fate.

"I am definitely guilty of second-degree murder," Sheena said in an interview around the time of her appeal.

But whether or not her appeals would be successful, she felt all along that she could never be free. "For somebody with a case like this, the prison is not really the prison. It's always going to be inside. You will always be in prison. It does not matter whether you are free or locked up, I think you will always have that inside."

But on Tuesday 25th July, that year, the Missouri Supreme Court returned the unanimous verdict that her appeal did not stand. Based on the facts of the case, they still argued that it was necessary for Sheena to be imprisoned for life.

Sheena's final hearing

It turned out that Sheena would eventually win her appeal after all.

In 2015, Sheena appealed again, under the same Supreme Court ruling as before. In her hearing of October that year, she sought the sentence of second degree murder through a plea agreement with the prosecutor. To do so, Eastburn had to waive any and all post-conviction and appeal rights- which she did.

The hearing was only 25 minutes long in total this time around. Lou Kelling, a former sheriff and supporter of Eastburn's release on parole, said at the appeal, "This is what she should have been charged with to begin with. She was an accessory to the crime. She served 10 years more time than she should have served. That on top of the fact that she was mistreated while in custody."

The defence had indeed used the same arguments as in the prior appeal, including the evidence of Sheena's IQ test, and allegations of rape and forced abortion. This time, the court decided to vacate the prior judgement. Since she had been in prison for more than 23 years, the agreement made her immediately eligible for a parole hearing.

Parole at last

Sheena Eastburn is now set to be released from prison in November, 2017. She has been judged to have served her time for second degree murder, and is getting ready for life on the outside for the first time in her life as an adult.

In a telephone interview with the Joplin Globe after it became common knowledge that she was set to be released, Eastburn said: "I now know when I will be able to move on with my life. I am grateful for a chance at parole."

In the same interview, she described how she was planning to write to the parole board and the governor in the hope that she could demonstrate just how much she had changed during her time locked away from society. "I want to show that I can be successful outside of the prison," she said. "I am very sorry for the things that happened. I have changed my life and will make better choices."

In another interview, she described her plans for the outside world. "I would go to school to become a certified personal trainer. I would love to minister to juveniles and help them know that the choices we do make have a consequence. I really do want to help people. I know that sounds crazy. But I want to help and let them know there are other choices out there no matter what your life is like because I had a bad life and childhood, but I still had choices. I did not realize that then."

And it did indeed seem that she had made genuine effort to turn her life around. In a separate interview, Sheena's mother claimed that her daughter had made every effort she possibly could from within the prison system. "Sheena has completed all of the classes that they offer at the prison. She has taken everything ... She'll sit there and the taxpayers will pay $80,000 a year to feed and house her. If she had been let out, she'd have a job and feed herself. This is something I don't understand. But we are still grateful to have a release date."

"We have waited a long time for this day to come, but we don't know when she will be released. We don't have an out day yet," Blevins said. "It could be just a matter of some paperwork. No one can really say right now."

During her time in prison, Sheena had begun full time work as an obedience trainer for rescue dogs. On top of this full time job, she had also become a qualified aerobics instructor, and found occasional work in prison helping disabled inmates. On occasion, she even led victim counselling sessions. She had spent her time as wisely as she could, and it had given her inspiration for her future release.

Before her first appeal on the unconstitutional nature of her sentence, her attorney had said "Maturity and education, things like that, should be taken into account and that's all we're really asking, that she be given the opportunity to prove to the parole board and other people that she deserves a second chance."

By the end of this year, she will be getting that chance.